I0145596

THE ULTIMATE ALLOWANCE

How to teach your children the 'wealth rules'

they need to grow up happy, healthy, wealthy and wise.

ELISABETH DONATI

FIRST EDITION

INNERWEALTH PUBLISHING CO.

A DIVISION OF CREATIVE WEALTH INTL, LLC

SANTA BARBARA, CALIFORNIA

THE ULTIMATE ALLOWANCE

InnerWealth Publishing, division of Creative Wealth Intl, LLC
135 Chapala Street • Santa Barbara, CA 93101
www.UltimateAllowanceBook.com/Toll Free: 800-928-1932

Copyright © 2008 by Elisabeth Donati
All rights reserved. No part of this book may be reproduced or transmitted in
any form or by any means, electronic or mechanical, including photocopying,
recording or by any information storage and retrieval system, without written
permission from the author, except for the inclusion of brief quotations in a
review.

Published in the United States
Library of Congress Control Number: 2008927992

Library of Congress Cataloging-in-Publication Data:
Donati, Elisabeth
The Ultimate Allowance: An amazing system that turn kids into self-reliant
adults.
Elisabeth Donati
Includes index.
1. Money   2. Parenting   3. Allowances   4. Finance, Personal
5. Family   6. Education

ISBN, PDF ed.   978-0-9774618-0-6
ISBN, Print ed.   978-0-9774618-1-3
First Edition

NOTE TO PURCHASER...

THE EBOOK VERSION OF THE ULTIMATE ALLOWANCE
IS COPYRIGHTED AND IS ONLY FOR SALE AT
ULTIMATEALLOWANCEBOOK.COM

IF THIS IS THE EBOOK VERSION AND YOU PURCHASED THIS
BOOK FROM A SITE OTHER THAN OURS, PLEASE LET US KNOW
WHERE AND YOU'LL GET A 5 DOLLAR CASH REWARD.

ENDORSEMENTS

"Most schools are not teaching children about money, and that concerns me. The Ultimate Allowance teaches kids how to be with money and make a difference at the same time. A 'must-read' for parents who truly want a bright future for their kids."

~MANNY GOLDMAN, AUTHOR, *THE POWER OF PERSONAL GROWTH*
FOUNDER, PERSONALGROWTH.COM

"Teaching kids that money doesn't just appear from the magic money machine (ATM) is a formidable lesson. By teaching children how money works, this invaluable lesson will stay with them for the rest of their lives. The more they learn, the less money mistakes they will make."

~DARA DUGUAY, DIRECTOR, CITI OFFICE OF FINANCIAL EDUCATION
FORMER DIRECTOR OF THE JUMP$TART COALITION FOR PERSONAL
FINANCIAL LITERACY

"The foundation of success is understanding money management. Finally there is a place for our children to go to learn about managing their money and building a foundation and psychology for wealth. This system can be a major factor in turning our younger generation into smart, financially-savvy business owners to build a solid foundation for future generations."

~CLINTON SWAINE, FOUNDER, FRONTIER TRAININGS

"The Ultimate Allowance is one of the most practical and life changing financial books any parent can read. If you want to learn a simple system that will transform your child's values around money, this is the # 1 resource for parents!"

– KIM DEEP, CMA, AUTHOR OF *CONDUCTOR KASH*
AND THE PROSPERITY EXPRESS AND OWNER, KIDZ MAKE CENTS

Endorsements (cont.)

A Salute to an extraordinary leader, dedicated humanitarian and a very special friend.

Elisabeth Donati has been a friend, mentor and blessing to me for almost seven years. Her dedication to the Financial Empowerment and Education of youth and adults always has me speechless and in AWE. For those who know me, being speechless for me is a rare experience. Miss E gives 150% of herself and draws that level of commitment from the hundreds of dedicated advisors, teachers and coaches who use the Creative Wealth and Camp Millionaire Curriculums across the nation and around the globe. The mission of Creative Wealth International is to teach thousands of people to take control of their financial lives and REACH FOR THE STARS!

The Ultimate Allowance will bring new insights for young people who are confronted every day with significant financial challenges but lack the knowledge and SKILLS to meet them. With the help of this insightful book, parents everywhere will be able to help their students gain the tools they need to "grow up happy, healthy, wealthy and wise." Thanks Elisabeth for another blessing.

~WILLIAM PROUTY, CBC CEC CLU RHU MBA PHD, DIRECTOR GLOBAL
ECONOMIC & WORKFORCE DEVELOPMENT COALITION

"The Ultimate Allowance is a must read for every parent who wants to see their kids succeed when it comes to money issues. My wife and I have 5 kids and we've really struggled with allowances over the years- nothing has ever seemed to really work. This book gives us renewed hope that we will be able to leave an amazing legacy for our kids and for future generations to come, which is really exciting to think about!"

~ CURTIS ARNOLD, FOUNDER, CARDRATINGS.COM,
AUTHOR OF *HOW YOU CAN PROFIT FROM CREDIT CARDS*

"The Ultimate Allowance shows parents how to turn powerful wealth creation skills into fun activities for kids. This book make lifelong money principles easier to grasp for the young mind; a fun way to look at the world is a way that sticks."

~ DR. BEN MACK, BEST SELLING AUTHOR OF
THINK TWO PRODUCTS AHEAD

TABLE OF CONTENTS

ABOUT THE AUTHOR

Elisabeth Donati has a knack for inviting people to think differently, inspiring them to improve the lives of others as well as their own.

Elisabeth created Camp Millionaire (originally called The Money Camp) as a means to give children of all ages the financial education she didn't receive as a child. She started her unique summer camp program in 2002 with the intent of simply teaching a local financial education camp to kids and teens. Yet, after just two years of successful summer programs, she started getting phone calls and emails from all across the US and almost every country in the world. She realized the lack of financial literacy was a global problem and as such, would need a very special type of program to solve.

Elisabeth is an expert in the field of financial education for kids ages 10 and up. Her programs use accelerated learning techniques and an experiential style of programming (i.e., games, activities, role-playing and contests) to keep the participants engaged, increase their retention and ensure that the campers have a great time learning about the often dry and taboo-ladened subject of money. "Financial freedom is your choice" is just one of the many sayings, slogans and principles her programs teach. Elisabeth's programs teach kids and adults time-tested personal money management skills and wealth creation principles in an environment that incorporates thinking, understanding and relevance. Every program begins by exploring how our financial thoughts, beliefs and attitudes relate to our future wealth potential and ends with the idea that investing in assets that produce passive income is the road to financial freedom for all.

Elisabeth graduated from Oregon State University in 1983 with a degree in Commercial/Industrial Fitness. Though the topic of her life's work has shifted from fitness, health and nutrition to money and wealth creation, her passion is still inspiring others to become independent and self-reliant. Her goal is to enlist people and organizations all over the globe to help in her quest to teach kids everywhere how to make, manage and multiply their money wisely.

FOREWORD

It's one thing to make mistakes with money as a child and be able to learn from them; it's totally another to make the same types of mistakes as an adult because these same mistakes often are accompanied by painful, long-lasting consequences.

This book is my gift to you and to every parents or guardians of the beautiful children in this world who are filled to the brim with potential and just need the tools to let it overflow into their lives.

I wrote this book because, as you'll learn, no one ever taught me about money, investing or financial freedom. The concept that I would have to grow up and someday be responsible for myself financially never occured to me...until I was 30 years old. At that time I remember one thing: being angry. Not really angry at anyone in particular, just angry that I hadn't been given the chance to learn about money early to I could apply those principles to preparing to become financially free. Heck, financial freedom wasn't a phrase I ever heard growing up and I would venture to say most adults don't hear as children.

You see, it's impossible to ask for answers to questions you don't know you have, until you trip over them one day. This is what happened to me.

One day, a long time ago, a friend gave me the amazing book, *Rich Dad Poor Dad*, by Robert Kiyosaki. I devoured the book in just two days, stunned by what I hadn't been taught, saddened by the financial potential I would never recover and desperate to somehow catch up; and lastly, committed to doing anything and everything I could to make it so kids the world over wouldn't have to experience what I had. As a straight A student in high school and college, I had a tough time reconciling the fact that I didn't know about money. Over time, though, I picked myself up, dusted off my feelings and set out to teach myself about this wonderful thing we call money.

I hope you enjoy the book and that it makes a difference in your life and the lives of your children.

DEDICATIONS

This book is dedicated to the people who have helped me build Creative Wealth's unique financial education programs beginning with the very first Money Camp for Kids (now Camp Millionaire) in the Fall of 2002. I'd also like to give a special thankyou to the people who have helped shape me into the person who could build it and then write this book. This is just a partial list of people I have to thank.

Walt Harasty, a retired business attorney, whose letter to the editor in 2001 hit me square in the face with a profound way to make a difference in people's lives: teach them how to become financially free. His letter asked, quite simply, "When are we going to start teaching our kids about money?" My answer? "Build the most amazing financial literacy camps for kids and teens the world would ever know!"

Larry Stein, who passed away in early 2007 at 58 years old, was my cofounder. His own lack of financial education allowed him to grasp the mission (which he helped create) and be supportive even when he became very sick and eventually lost his battle with cancer. I thank him and his amazing partner, Laura, for all their support over the years.

My mom, who taught me to be resourceful. She has no idea how I've depended on this skill during my short time on this earth.

My last husband, John Donati, who encouraged me from the get go and to this day, lends a helpful ear and support whenever I ask. If only all divorces could end this happily.

My best friend, Steve Gordon, who has been supportive beyond belief. He provides guidance when I ask, an ear when I don't, hugs when I need them, distinctions that allow me to see in entirely new ways and emergency infusions of sushi when I'm too tired to cook.

Robert Kiyosaki, who, through his book, *Rich Dad, Poor Dad*, showed me the first glimmer of how to be financially free.

T. Harv Eker for many things: the accelerated teaching techniques that make our programs so amazingly effective and fun; how to coach life into a person, and how to build a kid's seminar business like a pro.

The parents who have so blindly trusted us with their kids and their kid's futures. You have shared stories, happy and sad, tales of how our programs have affected your family and more. Thank you so much!

And finally, thanks to all my friends who support, listen, hug, celebrate and just show up when I need them, and even when I don't. I couldn't have done this without all of you.

Elisabeth, a.k.a., Miss E

NOTE ABOUT NAME CHANGES:

As of January 1, 2008, *The Money Camp* program that I mention throughout the book was renamed *Camp Millionaire* and the name of the Money Camp 501(c)(3) organization is now *Creative Wealth International*. The names were changed for the following reasons:

Though the name, *The Money Camp*, appealed to adults, parents and teachers, it never appealed to kids and teens. So, in order to get kids and teens to buy into the program *before* they attend and to make it easier for parents to enroll their kids in the program, the name was changed to *Camp Millionaire*. It's that age-old marketing idiom: sell them what they want, give them what they need!

The name of the organization was changed to Creative Wealth International to reflect both our international progress and goals and to highlight the fact that we teach individuals of all ages to use creativity and resources to become financially free sooner than later. This way they can live the lives they dream and have plenty of time to do a lot of good in the world.

ALLOWANCE STORIES FROM PARENTS

A couple of years ago, I asked all the wonderful people in my database to send me stories about their experiences with allowances: what worked, what didn't work, etc. I got tons of emails back with a myriad of ideas, stories of things they'd tried, and more. Mostly I got stories of what didn't work. You could tell that most parents were frustrated and had tried many types of allowance ideas, most to no avail. Here are a few of these stories. Read on and see if any of them ring a bell.

● ●

My daughter was never motivated with an allowance. We tried giving her one for taking the garbage out, cleaning her room, etc. None of this motivated her. I suppose she knew I would give her what she needed anyway. She never asks for an allowance but takes the garbage out every week without being asked and cleaning her room will never happen. She has gotten a part-time job, puts half away, uses her own money for movies, etc. Rarely does she ask for money. The only motivation was her grades. If she got certain grades she wanted the bucks! You figure it out!

— CATHY R.

● ●

My son is 13. He gets $10 a week in allowance (increases $2 with each birthday). We have a "direct deposit" system. He receives $5 and $5 goes into his savings account. He can use his savings for a large purchase and to buy Christmas gifts for family and friends. He spends most of it on the latter and has become quite adept at determining a list, shopping wisely, and still having some money left over.

— DE J.

● ●

We have never given our 10-year-old son an allowance. We own an apartment building and have a laundry room with a coin-op washer and dryer. Our son's "enterprise" is to go to the laundry room and make sure it is clean and to keep an eye on it. He gets paid $5 each time we go. If we go once a month, he gets $5 that month. If we go more often, he gets more. We have recently worked out an arrangement for him to own the machines himself. He is paying off the machines (a "loan") with the proceeds from the machines and still keeps $5 for himself. He is learning about leverage because it is the tenants who are paying for the machines when they use them.

11

THE ULTIMATE ALLOWANCE

He is also learning the importance of keeping the laundry room clean and desirable for the tenants; he sees how people behave (some can be real slobs and don't care much about things they don't own) and he is seeing trends (the machines generate less income over the holidays when people go away).

—WENDY D.

• •

My children did not get allowances, but to earn money for Christmas presents for Mom and Dad, they were paid for different chores. They are now in their thirties and forties and still kid me about how little I gave them for cleaning the bottoms of my Revere Ware copper pans.

—VAL K.

• •

Don't know if this is relevant to USA, but our 12-year-old son receives £25 per month paid into his savings account. He says he is saving for a practice drum kit but whatever he decides, he will have to fund comics, sweets and PlayStation game rentals out of this account. He has to sign a book for any other money owed to him or owed by him (partly because his mother can never remember!). If he wants any extra money, he has to do chores to earn it. He gets an annual raise of £5 per month on his birthday.

Deducting money from his allowance for bad behaviour tends not to work as I cannot keep track of it! More effective is the threat of telling Grandma or confiscating his PlayStation for a set period of time, and being forbidden to go to archery classes!

—CLARE H.

• •

When my son turned 5-1/2, we started giving him $2.00 a week. We also started having him do a couple of weekly chores we thought he could handle. (I know attaching chores to getting an allowance is debatable, so we keep that connection vague but looming.) We make him put $1 in savings (permanent) and the other in a spending jar. He has been saving up to buy something. He was very gung ho at first, but now he is willing to surpass chores and allowance sometimes. It might be time to have him spend his money to see the fruits of his work.

—SUSIE M.

• •

I found when I gave my son an allowance, he 'expected' the money even if he did not do his chores. And it was always a battle, even if I kept a chore chart and proved that he hadn't done the work. So I eliminated allowance all together, BUT he still has chores. I find that I get better cooperation with getting his chores done without an allowance than when he was getting one. I don't know why. Maybe he thinks that I will reinstate it, but I'm not going to. I've decided that part of his [responsibility in] living here

12

is to pitch in and help, without compensation! This way he will (hopefully) help his wife around the house with things that need to be done, without expecting a reward!

—DENISE I.

We tried to dole out an allowance and it was too difficult to keep track of the process. My husband thinks that doing chores is part of living and participating in family life. The children should not receive a financial reward for daily tasks.

We tried to tie the allowance to non-chore related things like finishing homework without complaints; adding birdseed to the feeders without being asked to do it; getting all the morning, school-related papers, lunches, and sports gear in the car without being nagged; those sorts of things. Then we had to create a payment schedule that was balanced and appropriate to the task. This was so difficult. Both kids (girl 11, boy 9) felt that their contributions were more important and thus they were due more money. Ugh.

We created a chart/contract that the kids were to complete each week. Well, they'd forget and I'd forget and by Friday we were trying to remember "who did what" and it would become a series of disappointments. The other difficult determination was if a job was well done or not. Did a job that was sloppily completed mean partial payment? That was an argument waiting to happen.

One additional difficulty was having enough cash on Fridays. Some Fridays, I just didn't or couldn't get to an ATM or bank. So, we'd have to wait 'til Saturday. Well, Saturdays are busy and often we wouldn't get cash until Sunday. Then we're back to Monday and it all starts over again. Overall, for our family, it was just too difficult to manage.

One child, my daughter, couldn't care less about money. She has money all over her room. Doesn't care about it at all. It's inconsequential. My son, REALLY cares about money. He's extremely focused on spending, not saving.

So, our compromise is this. They receive money as gifts for birthdays, etc. Half of the money goes into their savings accounts. The other half they may spend. They also earn money in the neighborhood by feeding the neighbor's animals when their owners are on vacation. That money is deposited into savings the same way birthday money is deposited.

This way, they have money to spend, immediately, or later. Those decisions are very instructive. My son bought a mouse, mouse house, water bottle, food, cage fluffy stuff, totalling $45.00. He lost the mouse ($1.29) within the week of purchase. The $45.00 was 2/3 of his savings. That was an important lesson.

—LAURA W.

DEFINITION OF MONEY

Money represents an exchange of energy and/or value. As an example, if I grow oranges and you make chairs and I trade you 100 oranges for 1 chair, we have, in essence, just exchanged each other's energy. We both decided that your chair is 'worth' 100 of my oranges. This is how value is determined.

We trade our time and energy for money and we pay money for things because of the perceived value we place upon those things.

DEFINITION OF FINANCIAL FREEDOM*

When the PASSIVE INCOME from your

ASSETS is greater than the

EXPENSES of your chosen lifestyle!

(In other words, when you have more money coming in each month than you have going out and you aren't having to work very hard bringing that money in.)

Do you want Financial Freedom...

...for your children?

...for yourself?

If you answered "YES" to these two questions, then this book is a must for your entire family.

*This definition of Financial Freedom is from the book, *Rich Dad, Poor Dad* by Robert Kiyosaki

Keep your Kids from Becoming a Financial Statistic!

"An investment in education always pays the best investment."
~ BENJAMIN FRANKLIN

We all know that many statistics are made, manipulated and molded to fit the agenda of the person or group creating those statistics. The financial literacy statistics below, however, do shed a light on the serious consequences of a society full of individuals not prepared with basic financial management and wealth creation principles.

- More young adults drop out of college because of financial problems than academic problems.

- In 2000, 78% of undergraduate students had credit cards and the average debt on those cards was $2,748, according to Nellie Mae, a student loan agency. In addition, one out of ten undergraduates owed more than $7,000.

- A recent survey by Sallie Mae found that more than half of all college students accumulated more than $5,000 in credit card debt while in school. Of the 13,000 respondents, one-third piled on more than $10,000. Only 19% said they did not acquire any credit card debt while in school.

- Credit card debt among Americans ages 18 to 24 has risen 104% in the last decade, according to Demos, a nonprofit research organization. (http://www.timesfreepress.com/absolutenm/templates/life.aspx?articleid=19178&zoneid=10)

- There are entire seminars that teach companies to market to your kids!

- The number of personal bankruptcy filings in the United States increased more than fivefold between 1980 and 2004. By then, more Americans were filing for bankruptcy than were graduating from college or getting divorced.

And these are just a few of the scary statistics must change.

THE FOLLOWING IS AN ARTICLE ON WWW.DAVERAMSEY.COM (DAVE RAMSEY IS A RADIO HOST WHO PROMOTES FINANCIAL LITERACY).

Vince called my radio show with a problem that has become a trend. He signed up for multiple credit cards during his sophomore year at college to get the free campus t-shirt. He wasn't going to use the cards unless there was an emergency, but there was an "emergency" every week, and soon he was $15,000 in debt. He couldn't make the payments, so he quit school to get a job. The problem was, without his degree, his earnings were minimal. Worse than that, he also had $27,000 in student loans. Student loans aren't payable while you are in school, but when you leave school by graduating or quitting, the payments begin.

Vince was one scared 21-year-old with $42,000 in debt but making only $15,000 per year. What's scary is that Vince is "typical." The American Bankruptcy Institute reveals that 19% of the people who filed for bankruptcy last year were college students. That means 1 in 5 bankruptcy filings were by very young people who started their lives as financial failures.

A DISTURBING POST ON A WEB SITE IN AUGUST 2007 FROM A COLLEGE STUDENT IN DEBT:

I'm a college student who's being 'pursued' by credit card debt. I have no income, no assets (I do have a car that was valued at $500 when I got it 2 years ago) and am living in my mother's basement, though I will be moving to the house of a friend in a month.

As of now, I only have my college loan money to pay my bills, and not nearly enough to take care of the credit card bills. I'm pretty sure I'm judgment proof, but I have no idea how that will help me when my mother is being harassed by phone calls whenever I'm not home.

I've been dealing with it well the past month since I attempted suicide in June (on my 21st birthday, of all days) after a breakdown over money, but I'm starting to get to that point again. I can't afford a lawyer, my parents are going through a divorce so they are unable to help, I have no other family members with income, and I'm taking care of my partner who's been unable to find work for 2 years.

I live in Michigan, where we currently have the highest unemployment rate in the country. I had a job for a while, until I was being told to work a day though my classes or I would be fired—like an idiot, I quit. I can't quit school without then adding my college loan payments into the equation.

I guess my biggest question would be—how the hell do I get through this without another suicide attempt?

NOTE: *I emailed him to offer suggestions but never heard back.*

My Request for Help

Please don't let your child end up as one of these statistics or the subject of one of these stories. College students would rather jump off a bridge than tell you they are in debt, so pay close attention to your son or daughter's actions and behaviors around money.

It doesn't take much to create this situation. A spring-break trip with friends, a closet full of cool clothes, some high-tech toys and voilà, they are in a financial mess they can't get out of.

It's been said that an ounce of prevention is worth a pound of cure. I'm convinced it applies here and the earlier the ounce of prevention is provided, the better.

We have a lot of work to do, but I have the utmost faith in our ability to turn this situation around.

My thank you for being the type of parent who cares enough about your child's well-being that you'll do whatever it takes to make sure he or she grows up happy, healthy, wealth and wise.

INTRODUCTION

"Imagination is the beginning of creation. You imagine what you desire,
you will what you imagine and at last you create what you will."
~ GEORGE BERNARD SHAW

In August of 2002, thirty-nine bright, young students, ages 9-14, attended the first *Money Camp for Kids* in Santa Barbara, California. For five days, they learned everything I could teach them about money, financial freedom and life in that hot, crowded upstairs room at one of our local Boys and Girls Clubs.

The Money Camp, now called *Camp Millionaire,* is a unique experience for kids and teens whose chances of being exposed to the essential financial information we teach are slim to none. The information and principles we teach in our programs helps ensure that they are able to live the lives they choose, not lives of quiet desperation, as too many adults live today.

Our Creative Wealth programs for adults are also unique in that we teach adults the same basic information we teach kids but we do it in a way that is fun and engaging and in an environment that is safe and full of encouragement and understanding.

The fact is, a huge percentage of adults have never been exposed to the critical financial information they need to live the lives they dream. Adults are hungry for this information and the skills needed to improve their lives. Men and women alike leave our programs saying they finally have 'hope' for a brighter future.

Even though financial literacy has become a hot topic these days in many state legislatures, it's still not a topic that is widely taught. For financial literacy information, statistics and legislation in your state, visit:

www.jumpstart.org/legislation.cfm

19

Though many states have passed bills requiring schools to teach financial literacy, finding the funding and training the people to promote and teach it frequently leaves these programs unimplemented or implemented very poorly. And though I am a bit biased, most of the programs I have seen would bore most kids to death.

Happily, more and more programs like *The Money Camp for Kids/ Teens* (Camp Millionaire and Moving Out!) are popping up each year, as communities begin to address the lack of financial literacy in their schools and neighborhoods. By reading and using the allowance system in this book, you are joining the ever-increasing ranks of parents who realize they can't depend on the 'system' to prepare their kids to handle money wisely. These parents, like you, have made a commitment to do whatever it takes to make sure your kids are prepared for life when they leave home.

WHY I WROTE THIS BOOK

I wrote this book for a couple of reasons. First, because I want to make sure as many kids as possible learn the financial skills they need to grow up happy, healthy, wealthy and wise.

I never got this information when I was a kid, or in my 20s, or even into my 30s! I was in my late 30s before I realized I had this HUGE gap in knowledge when it came to what to do with my money. After filling in this gap myself, I wanted to share it with as many parents as possible so they could share it with their kids.

Second, this book is my response to the overwhelming number of questions I've been asked about allowances since starting my financial education programs. Parents kept asking me, "So, what do you think about allowances?" All those questions caused me to go searching for answers.

Years of researching what the 'experts' thought and were doing with allowances helped me not only answer all the questions, but develop this amazing system that finally does what it's supposed to: prepare kids to handle money not just wisely, but brilliantly!

This book was written for you, the parent or guardian, for your children and for our nation, because it takes fiscally intelligent people to become fiscally responsible citizens.

HOW TO USE THIS BOOK

I suggest you first read the book yourself, and then, once you understand the system and have had a little time to do a bit of planning, share it with your children. This way your children feel like an active participant in understanding how the material in the book and the allowance system are relevant to their success with money, now and later on in life.

Remember, for your child, or anyone else, to be open to learning, the information presented must be relevant. Don't worry. Not only is this information extremely relevant, I've also created tools, games, and even scripted conversations for you to use to help you teach your child about money.

Because our programs teach so many powerful financial habits and principles, I decided it was time to write a book that includes these valuable lessons all in one place.

So, here it is. May it help you prepare your children for a lifetime of financial success and freedom!

WHY ALLOWANCES ARE IMPORTANT

"The best defense is a good offense."
~ DAN GABLE, OLYMPIC GOLD MEDALIST
AND MOST SUCCESSFUL COACH IN HISTORY

Imagine that your child wants to be a major league pitcher but you never giving him a ball to throw, a glove to catch with, never giving him time on the field to practice, oh yeah, never teaching him the rules. This is what money is like for most young adults. They are rarely given a chance to learn how to use it wisely. Most of them learn how to spend it really well. Spending it, however, doesn't lead to financial success or freedom!

Learning to do more than simply spend money is why providing your child with an allowance is so critical. Practice is how lessons are learned and habits are formed. One of our Creative Wealth Coaches uses the adage, "Repetition is the mother of skill." If this is true, and I believe it is, then only through the actual practice of using money will a child truly learn to use this resource wisely. That's why allowances are important. No practice, no lessons. No lessons, no skill. No skill, well . . . we know what happens when there's no skill. You have a society like ours that's deep in debt with no knowledge of how it got there or how to get out. I want to change this situation and I need your help!

MY GOALS FOR THIS BOOK

1) Provide you, the parent, grandparent, or guardian with a simple tool to prepare your child to use his financial resources wisely while, at the same time, use it to benefit his family, his community and, to a larger extent, the world around him.

2) Provide you with a way to reduce the stress and number of arguments you may have with your children.

3) Provide you with a way to reduce the amount of money it takes to raise a fiscally responsible adult.

23

4) Provide you with a sense of security that you are raising an adult (not a child) who will be able to take care of himself and his family after he leaves home. We don't want you to have to provide him with 'adult-child outpatient care.'

5) Provide you with the peace of mind that you're doing your very best to prepare him for a happy, healthy, wealthy and wise life. After he moves out, you can sit back and let him figure the rest of it out on his own.

6) And finally, my biggest goal of all: Provide you with the tools you need to help grow a new generation of adults who value balanced budgets (to become fiscally responsible politicians), a clean environment and opportunity for all.

BOOK NOTES:

1. The commonly accepted pronouns 'he' and 'she' are used interchangeably in this text for simplicity.

2. I use "I" when referring to my own opinions and ideas and "we" when I'm referring to *The Money Camp/Camp Millionaire* programs.

2. The Money Jar system used in this book is taught in Peak Potential's Millionaire Mind Intensive program and T. Harv Eker's book, *Secrets of the Millionaire Mind*.

3. There are many web-related resources listed in the book for more information on certain topics. At the time of this printing, all of the links were active.

4. I've created a place for you to jot down important notes at the end of many chapters for your convenience.

5. While reading this book, if you have any feelings of guilt or remorse, at having done something that may have caused difficulty for your child, or notice where your own parents might have done something differently and produced a different result for you, please vow right now to remember this principle, "People do the best they can with the information they have at the time." With

new information, we can learn, change our beliefs and behaviors and produce new results for ourselves and our children, and even for our parents at times.

CREATIVE WEALTH PRINCIPLES

Creative Wealth Principles are the sayings we use in our programs that represent the rules to the Money Game. To read them all, visit:

www.creativewealthintl.org/principles.php

The following are a few of the most basic financial principles your kids will learn by using the Ultimate Allowance:

- Life is a direct result of the choices we make.

- Our choices are influenced by our belief systems.

- You are the CEO of your own life.

- Money is a tool to reach your dreams.

- Pay yourself first.

- Save early, save often, invest wisely.

- Put your money to work for you.

- Great money habits create financial freedom.

- If you can't afford it in cash, you can't afford it at all.

- It's better to tell your money where to go than ask it where it went.

- Passive income is the key to financial freedom.

The principles are sprinkled throughout the book like this:

CREATIVE WEALTH PRINCIPLE
People Aren't Judged By Their Abilities, But By The Sum of Their Choices.

THE ULTIMATE ALLOWANCE

"Too many people are thinking of security instead of opportunity.
They seem to be more afraid of life than death."
~ JAMES F. BYMES

So, you're torn. Do you give your kids an allowance or not? And if you do give them an allowance, on what do you base it? When do you start giving it to them and how much do you give them?

Do you make them do chores? Do you reward them for good grades in school? Do you pay them for doing extra work around the house?

Do you let them spend it as they wish, or do you, in some way, control how the money is spent, saved, invested or given away?

These are just a few of the many questions parents frequently ask me about allowances. Parents tell me they just want their kids to understand the value of a buck, and the best ways to use it. If you're like most of the parents I talk to, you get a bit tired of your kids asking you for money all the time and wish there was a better way. I'm happy to report that there *absolutely* is a better way!

It is my experience that most parents want the best for their kids. When it comes to money, however, the challenge often lies in the fact that many parents weren't taught about money when *they* were young. If this is you, don't feel bad. You are not alone!

I understand why you struggle with finding the best ways to prepare your kids to handle money. How can you possibly teach something you don't know or aren't very good at yet? If you're struggling financially, teaching your kids is either the farthest thing from your mind or the foremost thing on your mind because you don't want the same thing to happen to them. We don't want our own children to have to learn the hard way.

27

Parents often say it's easier to talk to their kids about drugs or sex than money. The 'taboo' that shrouds the discussion of money can be extremely nerve-wracking. Just bringing up the subject can set off heightened and uncomfortable emotions of shame, embarrassment, anxiety and more. Your particular discomfort usually stems from how your own family dealt with the topics of money, wealth, paychecks, bills, investments, and anything else money-related.

If you *do* come from a family that had money, and your family has sufficient financial resources now, you may still struggle sometimes when it comes to teaching your kids about money.

My mom used to say, "You can't teach your own kids how to swim." I didn't understand what she meant until, at age 25, I had my son, Andrew (now a college graduate, debt-free and on his way to financial freedom . . . Yeah!). What I realized she meant was that children don't like listening to their own parents and often don't believe a word they say; at least, not until they mature a bit (I see you nodding your head in agreement). But they often believe what someone else tells them. It's amazing how smart my Mom became as I got older!

Regardless of how much they know about money and how it works, parents are often confused about the whole allowance issue for several reasons. First, they often relate back to their own experience of either getting or not getting an allowance as a child. It isn't always true that parents who received an allowance always give their children an allowance or that parents who didn't get one don't give one to their children. I have noticed over the years that what the parent experienced in terms of getting or not getting an allowance isn't always passed down.

It seems to be more about the *experience* the parent had around the allowance that dictates whether they give, and how they give, their children an allowance. Let's explore some of the more common allowance strategies before we move on.

CURRENT ALLOWANCE THEORIES

After doing quite a lot of research and talking to many parents over the past 6 years, I've noticed the following allowance approaches:

THE "NO ALLOWANCE AT ALL" CAMP

In my experience, parents in this camp usually didn't get an allowance when they were young. A common opinion is that if it was okay for them not to receive an allowance, then it's okay for their child not to receive one. Several parents I have talked to who felt this way seemed almost hostile and even angry, when the subject of allowances was brought up. They want their children to have to work for their money just like they did. They view the need for an allowance through their conditioning (in other words, how they were raised to see things), so they often just do with their children as their parents did with them.

Parents who feel this way are sometimes struggling with money and personal finances themselves. They are often very emotional about the financial issues in their lives so just talking about the concept of giving their child an allowance is often more than they can handle. If this is you, it's okay. Just stay with me here and you'll begin to understand.

Children who don't get an allowance sometimes develop a good work ethic, but they learn very little about money. They also tend to think that in order to have money they must always trade their time and energy for it. These children often don't learn how to manage, save or invest their money wisely. They can also grow up with the belief that they have to work 'hard' to make money, instead of learning that they can work 'smart' to make money. In addition, these kids can develop poor buying habits because they have little experience buying things for themselves on a regular basis.

Parents in this camp are often life-long employees or self-employed, always trading their time and energy for money. While there is nothing wrong with this lifestyle, it doesn't teach kids the importance of developing passive income streams by investing their money in assets (business, stock market and real estate). Not giving your kids a chance, from a young age, to take care of themselves financially, limits the amount of experience—positive and negative—they can have with their money. To a great extent, this experience then limits how prepared they are to successfully handle their own finances when they leave home.

THE "DOING CHORES ALLOWANCE" CAMP

Parents who require their kids to do chores around the house in exchange for an allowance tend to think that kids should 'earn' their allowance by 'doing' something. The only trouble with this concept is that it negates the idea that kids should participate as contributing members of the family by having certain duties and responsibilities that go along with being a family member; namely, keeping their rooms clean, helping out in the kitchen and yard, doing laundry, shopping, etc. These parents often provide a little 'extra' allowance for additional duties like washing the car or mowing the lawn.

The main disadvantage to this type of an allowance is that your kids may think they don't need to do their chores if they don't need the money. Paying kids for chores certainly doesn't teach them that making their beds is a great habit to get into every morning. If paying kids for doing chores worked, these kids would all grow up to be great housekeepers, but so far I think the jury is still out on that one! If you have ever visited kids in college and noticed the way they keep their dorm rooms, you might understand what I mean.

THE "PAYING FOR GRADES" CAMP

It's important to understand the difference between intrinsic and extrinsic rewards or motivation. Paying for grades seems like paying the child for behavior that is best for the parent, not necessarily best for the child. For a child who is already motivated to get good grades, dangling a financial reward for better grades may not have much of an effect on behavior. For a child who has no interest in school or getting good grades, the money may either motivate extrinsically and eventually create some intrinsic motivation, or it may cause exactly the opposite result. It may cause the child to become resentful of money in general, which can then lead to long-lasting negative financial beliefs that may affect his financial future. For deeper insight into this topic, please read, *Secrets of the Millionaire Mind,* by T. Harv Eker or visit:

www.peakpotentials.com/a/tofreedomandbeyond

We tend to equate a child's success in life with how well he does in school. However, there's no proof that this correlation is valid. There isn't any hard core proof that if they attend, or finish, college they will be more successful in life. Some of the most famous people in the world didn't even finish high school.

- Robert Frost was dropped from school for daydreaming. He was probably composing poems during some of his daydreams.

- Frank Lloyd Wright daydreamed so intensely that his uncle had to shout at him to bring him back.

- Thomas Edison was said to be "addled" because of his excessive daydreaming in class.

- Nikola Tesla had such strong visualization abilities that he would imagine the workings of his inventions in great detail without putting anything on paper or conducting any experiments until all of the problems were worked out.

For a more complete list of other famous people who suffered all sorts of problems related to their education and who later found success, visit this web site:

www.familyvillage.wisc.edu/general/famous.html

Traditional schools test for genius in only a few areas, mostly Logical-Mathematical, Verbal-Linguistic and sometimes Spatial-Visual. Genius, however, exists in many more areas. An inspiring book on accelerated teaching techniques, *Quantum Teaching,* by Bobbi DePorter, Mark Reardon and Sarah Singer-Nourie, describes the many varieties of genius.

We share these different kinds of genius with kids and parents in all of our programs because we want kids to know that they are *all* geniuses; they just have to find the genius in them. The main categories are:

- Spatial-Visual—thinking in images and pictures

- Linguistic—thinking in words

- Interpersonal—thinking by communicating with other people

- Musical-Rhythmic—thinking in rhythms and melodies

- Naturalist—thinking in reference to nature

- Bodily-Kinesthetic—thinking through physical sensation and movement

- Intrapersonal—thinking reflectively

- Logical-Mathematical—thinking by reasoning

For more information, or to give your child's teacher this amazing resource, visit:

www.creativewealthintl.org/accellearn.php

There are studies that show that the more schooling a person gets, the higher the salary they command; but remember, this correlation is only true for people who remain employees all their lives.

Nearly one-third of all high school students don't graduate and less than 50% of those that do aren't prepared for college. So the solution for these kids is not to pay them for grades but prepare them to use the one tool we know they'll have to use...money!

ALLOWANCE CONCLUSIONS

After teaching Money Camps for Kids and Teens for six years, and spending tens of thousands of dollars attending train-the-trainer, financial and personal growth seminars, I've come to the following three conclusions regarding kids and allowances:

CONCLUSION #1:

An allowance, just like most things in life, can be a good thing or a not-so-good thing. It can motivate or demotivate. It can be supportive or unsupportive. It can create self-reliance or dependence. It all depends on how you use it, how you and your child interpret it and the experience your family has around it. The end result from any type of allowance varies with each child. Just like no two children are alike, neither is the end result when using an allowance, at least the types of allowances we've talked about so far.

CONCLUSION #2:

Almost all children, regardless of age, understand the difference between spending *your* money and spending *their* money. Yours is generally much easier to spend!

CONCLUSION #3:

If children are empowered with the information, tools and responsibility of learning how money works, along with the encouragement to establish a few simple but powerful money habits, they generally grow up to be much more financially responsible than children who do not receive this education.

Though all three conclusions are important, Conclusion #3 is what led me to develop this allowance system.

If a child isn't given the information, tools and responsibility of handling money when she is young, including opportunities to have success with it, find pleasure in it and make painful mistakes with it, that child often grows up to be an adult who just doesn't have a clue what to do with money when she starts earning it herself. To her, money is just a tool to buy *piddlyjunk** as we call it in our camps (see definition on following page).

If a child has just one negative experience with money, and no structured financial experience or education to offset it, this one negative experience can set him up for a lifetime of financial misery. It doesn't have to be this way! Learning to manage money should not be left to chance and it definitely should not be an elective in school.

If children are exposed to, and practice, positive money habits when they are young, they have a pretty easy time maintaining those positive financial habits as adults. With a few basic, time-tested money-management skills and wealth-creation principles under their belts, they will have an easier time becoming *financially free**!

*Piddlyjunk: Something you buy that either goes *down* in value after you buy it (clothes, CDs, games, etc.) or has *no* value after you buy it, (e.g., consumables; eating out and buying junk food and coffee fit that bill quite nicely). If you go out every day for coffee, you are literally drinking your retirement and eating up the funds you could be using to create financial security for yourself. For a great book on how a little money adds up to riches over time, read, *Smart People Finish Rich*, by David Bach. Be forewarned you will probably be tempted to give up that morning coffee at your favorite coffee house after you read this book, but I promise it's a good thing.

*Financially free: You are financially free when the *passive income* from your investments (assets) exceeds the *expenses* of your chosen lifestyle. It's not necessarily true that you have to be rich to be financially free. A better theory, one most people find easier to swallow, is to get free financially first and become rich later! Just imagine how much more *good* we can do in the world and how much more enjoyment we'll get from our lives if we become financially free at an earlier age.

Let's look deeper into my three conclusions.

ALLOWANCE: GOOD OR BAD?

If you give your children money for no other reason than to have money to spend, what do they usually do with it? They spend it! Not always, but more often than not, kids like to spend the money they get (just like we do, or would love to do if we didn't have to be so responsible). There is a certain type of child, however, that won't spend money, no matter how much he has. If you have one of these, don't think you don't have work to do. This kind of child often grows into an adult who hoards his money or who doesn't enjoy his money and that's not healthy either.

Let's talk about the concept of delayed gratification for a bit. In the article, *Why Johnny Can't Save for Retirement,* (Fortune Magazine, April 2004), author Justin Fox talks about two very different brain functions: the primal function of the limbic system, which developed long before there was money, malls, credit cards or catalogs, and the cognitive, contemplative function of the prefrontal cortex, which is always busy calculating and weighing options. A study cited in the article found that when students were given the option of taking a specific sum of money now, or receiving a larger sum of money later, most of them chose taking the money now, and when they did this, their limbic systems (i.e., the primal brain) lit up like Christmas trees!

You see, we are hard wired for survival. This used to mean that we got excited when a deer walked past us because it represented food and, therefore, survival. This doesn't happen much anymore, unless you live in Virginia, where many businesses actually give their employees the first day of deer season off as an 'official' vacation! Generally speaking, Americans are pretty close to a grocery store most of the time. If not, the local 7-Eleven is full of tempting, hunger-satisfying, albeit life-shortening treats.

So there's actually a biological reason why we spend the money we get as soon as we get it, and this may explain why we buy things we may not necessarily need or want. Let's look at ways to teach this ever-elusive concept of delayed gratification, as it appears to be an acquired skill, and a valuable one at that.

In Carla Hanniford's book, *Smart Moves*, she discusses delayed gratification in terms of the developing emotions of a child. She suggests playing a simple time game when children are young (about 3 years old). For example, when a child asks for a snack, say, "Sure, and I will give it to you in three minutes." Then set an egg timer and ask the child to let you know when it's time. When the timer goes off, and the child lets you know, give the child the snack. She says that when children know their needs will be met, they easily develop a sense of time and learn delayed gratification.

35

What do children learn if you just give them an allowance but don't tie it to lessons, responsibility, choice, self-reliance and more? Absolutely nothing. At least nothing tangible in terms of helping them establish meaningful financial habits that will take them into adulthood.

Again, if you pay your children to do chores around the house, you are in essence paying them to do things that they should be doing simply because they are contributing members of the household. We all want to provide valuable lessons for our children through the activities we have them do. The most this kind of allowance usually accomplishes, however, is to encourage them to be good at making their beds or putting away the dishes.

Making kids do chores for money can also make them resentful because in order for them to get money from you they have to perform

tasks that they may not necessarily feel like they should be doing. This type of an allowance, unless there are some rules or guidelines in place about what the child does with the money, rarely teaches the necessary skills or the financial discipline they will need as adults.

If you give your children money for doing chores, and you *do* give them rules about *how* they have to allocate this money, and if you do so without the *why*, your child may also develop negative feelings and emotions about money and this may cause them to be even more resentful. Resentment is not a healthy emotion to have about money yet it is a common emotion that adults feel toward money, and it usually develops in childhood through the experiences a person has with money.

Lawrence Stein, the man who helped launch The Money Camp, always shared his story about why the 'why' is so critical. He said his mother always told him to just put away $50 a month. However, when he added it up ($50 x 12 months x 50 years), it only amounted to $30,000. Even as a teen he knew he couldn't retire and live comfortably on that sum so he just concluded that he'd save money when he started earning more of it. Makes sense, right? It's easy to see how he came to that conclusion.

What his mother left out, however, was the *why*. She never showed him what would happen to his money over the long run if he invested it wisely (put it to work) so that it made money for him. Had she added a simple conversation about compound interest and compound growth, he may have been a bit more motivated to save the $50 every month. He would have had his 'why.'

Let's look at a common example that you could use with your child. If Larry had actually invested that $50 every month in the stock market for 50 years and gotten a 10% return on his investment (also called his ROI), he would have had *$873,488.04*. That sum would have gotten his attention! For a simple chart on how compound interest works, see page 180. For a great simple calculator on the web, visit:

www.planningtips.com/cgi-bin/savings.pl

If, however, you provide opportunities for your child to earn money for doing things that are what most of us consider "above and beyond the call of duty"— things like washing the car or mowing the lawn, cleaning out the gutters — then you are instilling a work ethic that may prove valuable in the future. This is a good thing.

SPENDING YOUR MONEY, NOT THEIRS

Many of you may have already noticed that when you offer to buy something for your child, he or she is usually eager to let you do it. Often this eagerness has little to do with how much the child actually wants the thing you're offering to buy. He is just excited because it's always fun to get new things, especially when someone else is paying.

However, when it comes to spending *their* money, it's a completely different story! If I may, let me tell you how I figured this one out on my own.

Many years ago, when my son Andrew was a teenager, he became so hard to buy gifts for that I got in the habit of just giving him money to buy his own gifts. We'd then schedule a shopping trip so he could buy something he wanted. He usually wanted clothes so we'd end up in a department store or a mall, walking from here to there, comparing

prices, talking about whether a particular pair of jeans was worth $40, whether he wanted or needed new underwear. You get the picture.

One afternoon, a couple of days after Christmas, he and I were having this annual exhausting experience and after a few hours I couldn't take it anymore. He simply couldn't decide what, if anything, he really wanted. I got frustrated, reached into my wallet, pulled out a nice crisp $100 bill and handed it to him. I said, "Here, buy whatever you want." He took the bill, looked at it, looked at me, put the bill in his pocket and replied nonchalantly, "Let's go home. I really don't want anything."

I was speechless! What had just happened? More importantly, what had I just learned? I realized then and there that it's easier to spend someone else's money than it is to spend our own. From that point on, things became much easier financially between my son and I. Today he is financially self-sufficient, uses credit cards wisely (he has one that awards points and he pays it off every single month), and regularly puts money into his ROTH IRA, which his Dad and I helped seed, of course. I'm proud to say, I practiced what I preach with him and, more importantly, I can say that it works.

NOTE: I didn't use this type of allowance with my son since it didn't exist then and I had no idea what I didn't know back then. He did get an allowance, however, and quite a lot of coaching from his father and I, and I know that helped get him to where he is today.

TEACH THEM NOW...OR LIVE WITH THEM LATER

Financial responsibility in adulthood happens quite naturally if sound financial habits are established early in life. According to the National Endowment for Financial Education (NEFE), as few as ten hours of classroom instruction can be enough to persuade students to improve their spending and saving habits. Considering the amount of time most kids spend watching TV in one week, ten hours isn't very much to ask of them.

Current statistics paint a dismal picture in regard to young adults' financial situations, and more importantly, their financial futures.

More college students leave school now because of financial problems than because of academic reasons. Many college students graduate these days burdened with often insurmountable debt, frequently forcing them to move home because they simply can't make it on their own.

These kids can easily fall into depression over the debt they have often unknowingly created and are even committing suicide over this debt. Many 20-somethings are simply unable to cope with the debt they are getting themselves into during college. This is a terrible way to start their new lives after they graduate, *if* they graduate at all.

There is something dreadfully wrong with this situation, but you can prevent this from happening to your child. Simply prepare them now!

NOTES:

WHO'S TO BLAME

"To err is human; to blame the next even more so."
~ UNKNOWN

We could point the finger of blame in many directions. Instead, let's look at the question in terms of who is responsible for preparing children for adulthood in whatever area we might choose; money, relationships, communication, job skills, health, social responsibility and more. I'd like to suggest that rather than getting all huffy about what 'should' be, we take a simple look at what *is* and see how we can all help to improve the situation. I once heard a wonderful quotation at a seminar that has stuck with me:

"The world won't change until we stop fighting against that which is wrong and start promoting that which is right." Now, even though right and wrong and good and bad will always be subjective things, we can apply that quotation here and stop fighting but rather begin promoting different aspects of educating our kids about money.

PARENTS

I think we can all agree that the primary responsibility for raising fiscally responsible adults lies with the parents. At least that's where we start. As I've already suggested, the challenge lies in the fact that so many parents simply don't know what or how to teach their kids about money because *they* don't know about money themselves.

SCHOOLS

We could look next to formal education and ask our schools and teachers to provide our kids with a financial education. Even though we'd all love to drop our kids off at school and have them fully prepared for adulthood between the hours of 8 and 3, it simply isn't happening. One statistic I read said that fewer than 10% of our high school graduates receive any kind of financial education, but I've also read that the majority of math teachers were indeed teaching aspects of financial literacy in their classes. Even if they

41

are learning something about money in school, most don't learn the critical information they need to grow into financially free adults. In general, our kids are earning diplomas full of irrelevant information that doesn't help them become successful in life. With all the well-meaning government standards, and the requirements that go along with them, there seems little room for essential life-skills information in the areas of financial literacy, communication, relationships, parenting, etc. If you scrutinize the No Child Left Behind Act, you'll see that it has left many a child behind.

Because schools are publicly funded, they have to do what they are told in order to get the money they need to continue operating. Even though financial literacy is included in the No Child Left Behind Act, after all is said and done, it doesn't appear to be included in most school curriculums on a regular basis yet.

Now, add to this equation a nation full of overworked, underpaid teachers who 'do it for the love of teaching' (i.e., not the money) and who also were not raised to be financially savvy; too many administrative staff, who also lack the financial education (and perhaps the will) to change the way they allocate resources and you end up with our current system where kids are not learning the things they absolutely must learn to be happy, successful adults. Bottom line: most schools claim they just don't have the necessary resources to teach kids about money. There are many teachers who *do* see the need for financial literacy and even have the desire to teach it; the system just doesn't make it easy for these teachers to teach it outside the normal curriculum.

When kids do get a bit of financial education, it is usually in the area of saving, writing checks, and perhaps, a little budgeting. There's rarely talk of creating financial freedom. Most financial education is focused on saving, then investing with compound interest (which is rarely how people become rich) and accumulating money over the long haul to retire when they're old. Our current system is set up to create employees and soldiers, not happy, financially free adults who could do a lot of good in the world if they had more than enough money to take care of themselves.

GOVERNMENT

Let's look next at the idea that it is our government's responsibility to make sure we're prepared to handle money wisely. I'm sorry to be so cynical here, but this would be like asking someone who can't swim to stand in as lifeguard at a local beach that's known for its riptides and sharks. Or better yet, asking someone who is petrified of public speaking to get up in front of 10,000 people to do a presentation on a subject they not only don't understand but aren't able to do themselves!

At this point, I'll defer to one of my mother's favorite sayings. Though, as an adult, I've learned that it doesn't always apply to creating success in life, in this case I think it's applicable:

"If you want something done right, do it yourself."

Parents: that means *you*. So, on that note, let's move on. We have adults to grow!

NOTES:

THREE SIMPLE THINGS YOU CAN DO TO EMPOWER YOUR CHILDREN FINANCIALLY

"We are the opening verse of the opening page of the chapter of endless possibilities." —RUDYARD KIPLING

There are three relatively easy things you can do to empower your children financially. These three things will provide them with the experience and information they need to grow up financially savvy. At the very least, they will be able to fend for themselves once they leave that safe little nest you've been providing for them. At the very best, they will grow wealthy and help others along the way.

If you do these three things, though I can't guarantee it completely, I can say with certainty that you will have done a tremendous service toward helping to prevent your child from becoming one of the statistics in the front of this book. These three things will prepare them to handle money wisely, as well as enable them to create financial freedom for themselves sooner rather than later.

Many parents say one of the reasons they send their kids to our camps is so that there will be someone to take care of them when they get older! Most parents say it with a grin, but I get the feeling that some of them are quite serious!

HOW WE LEARN

Before we move on, I want to share with you some interesting information about how human beings learn. This diversion is relevant because if you can present the information in this book, or any information for that matter, in a way your child learns best, it will be more powerful and effective.

How many of you were ever taught how learning happens? Or more to the point, how YOU learn? I find it interesting that we throw young children into classrooms with teachers, yet rarely ever do we have a conversation with them about the 'learning' part of learning.

45

There are three primary ways by which human beings learn. They are:

1) From the things we see (and read)—we call this VISUAL

2) From the things we hear (and say)—we call this AUDITORY

3) From the things we experience (and feel)—we call this KINESTHETIC

Visual   Auditory   Kinesthetic

Experts often refer to these learning modalities as **VAK**. Generally, teachers who use all three in their lessons are more effective teachers and their students have a much more enjoyable learning experience. Using these three modalities helps engage children in the learning process, rather than just forcing them to memorize often useless information they may never use.

A high percentage of teachers have been taught to use the auditory mode as the primary method of teaching. In other words, to stand in front of their students and talk to them. Thankfully, this is beginning to change. The challenge with using primarily auditory teaching methods is that only a small percentage of us are purely auditory learners. Most of us are either visual, kinesthetic, a combination of visual and kinesthetic, or a combination of all three. This variance in learning style may be one of the reasons why there are so many children and adults labeled with learning disabilities in this country. I don't believe there are many children with true learning disabilities. I do believe there are plenty of teachers with teaching disabilities, not because they are bad teachers, but because they simply weren't taught how to teach using all three learning styles.

NOTE: I do not say this with any disrespect for teachers because, after teaching children for six years, I understand how demanding teaching is these days. What I mean is, the standard method of teaching—sitting children, especially boys, behind desks and talking to them from the front of the classroom, expecting them to learn information that just isn't relevant to them yet—simply isn't very effective for most children or adults. And honestly, I think it's actually disrespectful. I do understand, also, the frustration most teachers live with nowadays due to the constraints of standards and administrations butting their heads in where they don't belong.

Imagine how controlled and angry you would feel if you were a profoundly effective teacher with many years of experience and your principal comes in one day and tells you you have to start teaching from a script? This is just one example of why our American schools, in general, receive such a poor grade.

Teachers who use Accelerated Learning Techniques teach to all three (3) learning styles at the same time; this method of teaching is incredibly more effective than lecture-style teaching. We've all endured occasions where a teacher or presenter stood before us and talked and talked and talked. What most of us remember is how bored and tired we felt.

With accelerated learning (the style we use in all of our financial programs, regardless of age), participants learn by seeing, saying, playing, competing and doing; we use music and games and activities that engage participants while they learn. And we do our best to make the information relevant. You're going to have to do the same thing when you teach your child the Ultimate Allowance system. Just remember, I'm going to guide you every step of the way. First, here are a few guidelines related to the three learning styles:

You know you are a VISUAL learner if someone tries to give you directions verbally and you just can't follow them. You ask them to draw you a map. You use words like, 'I see,' 'Tell me what that looks like to you' and 'I can see that working.' You prefer learning with picture, drawings, color, etc.

You know you are an AUDITORY learner if you can learn and remember anything from what you hear or read, and you don't have to be looking at the source or the teacher. You are the person who doodles or knits in class; you're simply focused on listening. You are getting it; you simply don't need to see to learn. You use words like, 'that sounds good to me' or 'I hear what you're saying.' You learn well through reading.

You know you are KINESTHETIC if you tend to look down and check in with your gut; in other words, you ask yourself how you feel about something inside. Remember, kinesthetic is both movement and emotion. You are kinesthetic if you have to experience it yourself in order to 'get it.' You use words like, 'I'm not sure how I feel about that,' or "I don't get a sense that that would work."

These are generalities, but they illustrate the idea. For more information on accelerated teaching and learning, read *Quantum Teaching* by Bobbi DePorter, Mark Reardon and Sarah Singer-Nourie, or *Smart Moves* by Darla Hanniford, both available at:

www.creativewealthintl.org/accellearn.php

There is a great camp program that uses accelerated learning called *Supercamp* for kids who are having difficulties in school. Once kids are exposed to this teaching style, they often realize there's nothing wrong with them; the problem lies in how they are being taught.

www.supercamp.com

FINALLY, THE THREE THINGS

"It has long been an axiom of mine that the little things are infinitely the most important."

~ SIR ARTHUR CONAN DOYLE (SHERLOCK HOLMES)

With this basic introduction into how humans learn, and perhaps a little insight into your own learning style, let's explore the three things you can do to prepare your kids for financial freedom (so they can support you when you're older ☺).

1st: Set the best example you can.

2nd: Make money a family matter.

3rd: Put your child in charge of his own finances.

1ST: SET THE BEST EXAMPLE YOU CAN

How many of you would agree that human beings learn best by example? Even though our parents often tried to teach us using the "Do as I say, not as I do" method of child rearing, we rarely listened. We know full well that kids often end up doing things exactly as they saw their parents doing them. Why wouldn't they? Another primary, though sometimes painful, way we learn is by making mistakes; in other words, by making poor choices. We'll talk about that in a bit.

Now that you understand the three primary ways we learn, you can see that your children are constantly watching and learning, consciously and subconsciously, from what you DO with money, what you SAY about money and from the EXPERIENCES you're providing them with regard to money. Your children are also learning from the other people they spend time with: step-parents, grandparents, aunts, uncles, teachers, friends and neighbors and let's not forget that big one...the MEDIA!

Let's make this part interactive, shall we? Take a few minutes and do this next section with your child. Answer the questions honestly and allow your child to answer the questions without judging him or becoming defensive. Keep in mind that this is a learning experience for everyone. In order for your child to develop a healthy relationship with money, he must feel safe (i.e., accepted and free of the need to provide answers he thinks you want to hear) around the topic of money. It's your job to provide that safe place.

If you have emotional reactions to some of these questions, I urge you to read the book, *Secrets of the Millionaire Mind*, by T. Harv Eker. It is the best book on belief systems I've ever read and it's required reading for all of my Success Calls Coaching clients. It's that powerful.

So, are you ready? Let's go. Remember, if you don't do the exercises, you won't learn anything. Get your favorite pen and take some time to really think about the questions before you answer them.

The first three questions relate to what you **do** with money.

1) What do I do on a regular basis that may be teaching my child something positive in regard to money?

_____

_____

_____

_____

_____

2) What do I do that may be teaching him or her something negative in regard to money?

_____

_____

_____

_____

_____

3) **[ask child]** What have you learned about money from watching me handle money?

_____

_____

_____

_____

_____

The next three questions ask the previous questions in terms of what you **say** about money.

4) What do I say on a regular basis that may be teaching my child something positive in regard to money?

_____

_____

_____

_____

_____

5) What do I say that may be teaching him or her something negative in regard to money?

_____
_____
_____
_____
_____

6) **[ask child]** What have you learned about money from listening to me talk about money?

_____
_____
_____
_____
_____

Let's explore your contribution to your child's **experience** around money.

7) What kinds of experiences have I provided for my child (on purpose or by accident) on a regular basis that may be teaching my child something positive in regard to money?

_____
_____
_____
_____
_____

8) What kinds of experiences have I provided for my child (on purpose or by accident) that may be teaching him or her something negative in regard to money?

_____
_____
_____
_____
_____

9) **[ask child]** Do you remember any experiences you've had with money that have been positive (happy, joyful) for you?

_____

_____

_____

_____

_____

10) **[ask child]** What did you learn from that (those) experience(s)?

_____

_____

_____

_____

_____

11) **[ask child]** Do you remember any experiences you've had with money that have been negative (unhappy, causing stress, etc.) for you or your friends?

_____

_____

_____

_____

_____

12) **[ask child]** What did you take away from that experience about money?

_____

_____

_____

_____

_____

As you can see from answering these questions is that it's what you've learned to make money *mean* that creates your entire experience around money (or any subject for that matter).

You see, it works like this: our thought patterns and behaviors start being formed (conditioned, rather) from an early age from a zillion different sources: parents, relatives, teachers, media, books, movies, news, music, drugs, food, exercise, experiences and more. As we are conditioned, we form 'opinions' of what is true and not true for us about everything: family, love, friends, work, life, happiness and yes, money. This conditioning runs our entire lives like an autopilot system unless and until we begin to understand it for what it is...just conditioning. In order to change how we think and behave in any area of our lives, we must begin to understand our conditioning. We often refer to this conditioning as our Belief System.

As one our Creative Wealth Coaches has pointed out, "Look at the first letters in the phrase Belief System." That kind of says it all! The sad thing? Most of our financial beliefs aren't ones we have chosen for ourselves. In other words, they aren't even ours!

It's important that we start to understand how, as parents and guardians, we influence our children's financial futures simply by the things we do, say and cause our children to experience around money. This influence leads our child to develop a financial mind-set that either supports him in his future or leads him to struggle forever with money.

Bottom line? Watch yourself, and know that your child is watching you also.

CREATIVE WEALTH PRINCIPLE

Your Thoughts, Beliefs and Attitudes
Determine Your Wealth Potential

UNCONSCIOUS STEREOTYPES THAT CONTROL US

Often the invisible is more powerful than the visible. Hopefully you have noticed that there are a lot of important things going on *underneath* the surface that actually control what we do *on* the surface. You can liken this relationship of the invisible to the visible to a tree and its root system. If a tree develops a solid, healthy root structure that goes down to an abundant supply of water and nutrients, the tree grows strong and tall. If it can't grow deep roots and doesn't get those nutrients, the tree is unstable and doesn't grow well. Human beings are no different. With proper physical and mental nutrients, they become strong. With improper nutrients, they become weak. It's that simple.

If you can see your life as having four distinct, important areas—physical, mental, emotional and spiritual—you begin to notice that the three areas you *can't* see shape the part you *can* see. I guess we could say that life is, in essence, 'an inside job!'

Let's have some fun! Please do this next activity with your child. Without much thinking, finish the following sentences, listing as many words or phrases as you can.

Rich people are (for example: snobby, smart):

_____

_____

_____

_____

_____

_____

_____

_____

_____

_____

_____

_____

_____

Poor people are (example: lazy, smelly, stupid):

Now look back at the Rich People list. Pick a word or phrase with a negative connotation. Would you want people to think of you this way? Why not? If you truly believed rich people to be greedy or stingy or mean, this unconscious belief could act to keep you from accumulating much money in your life because, after all, most of us don't want to be thought of as greedy or stingy or mean or any of the other negative traits you named.

Now look at the Poor People list. Again, choose a word or phase with a negative connotation. Would you ever want to help someone you thought of as having this trait (lazy, stupid, uncaring)? Now consider what type of people really need our help the most. People with little or no money are often (but not always) lacking the skills and knowledge to better themselves, yet our unconscious beliefs influence us here as well.

We want kids to understand that rich people aren't necessarily greedy and poor people aren't necessarily lazy. *Rich* people are rich and *poor* people are poor. *Greedy* people are greedy and *lazy* people are lazy! I personally know some extremely generous rich people and some very hardworking poor people.

Bottom line? Money only makes you more of what you already are.

INTRODUCING THE MONEY ANIMALS

Most of us understand the meaning of the word *personality*. We develop different personalities that we use throughout our lives, and throughout each day, for survival. We use different personalities as defense mechanisms, to impress others, to make us feel good, to help us cope with certain situations, etc. Many of us have developed very supportive personalities as well as some that aren't quite so supportive.

Believe it or not, we have all developed a *money* personality as well, and learning about these money personalities is important when you're exploring how you and your child deal with money.

There are six basic money personalities[1]. They are: the Saver, the Spender, the Avoider, the Monk, the Amasser and the Worrier *(see the complete list of money personalities on page 175)*. It's important to understand how money personalities develop. The age-old question of nature versus nurture plays a role here. Many parents with more than one child have told me they have a spender, a saver and an avoider and yet they swear they treated all three children the same with regard to money and finances. They shake their heads, not understanding how three children raised in the exact same environment can end up with completely different thought patterns and behaviors around money.

Personally, I think a child's money personality is determined a lot by nature with a healthy dose of nurture thrown in. If the scenario above is you, and you do a little honest digging through your memory, you may begin to notice that you were in slightly different financial situations with each child; perhaps becoming increasingly financially savvy and stable as each child was born or progressively under more financial stress. Though it may not seem different to you, the subtleties of every change over the years causes a change in the energy of the household; attitudes shift, language changes and each child is then exposed to a slightly different version of Mom and Dad and money. In addition, don't forget the powerful effect of the mother's emotional state during pregnancy.

---

1   Coined by Olivia Mellan (*Money Harmony: Resolving Money Conflicts In Your Life and Relationships,* Walker and Company, 1995).

If you consider that each individual is born with his or her own set of psychological tendencies (extrovert, introvert, etc.), you can see how each person in a family may develop a completely different and unique money personality within the same financial environment.

Our experience has shown that children as young as three years of age have started to develop their own financial personalities. Once a money personality has started to develop, children see everything from that point of view and through that conditioning.

How conditioning affects our financial lives is fascinating and how this conditioning contributes to all other areas of our lives is even more interesting. For a great book on the subject of conditioning, please read, *How to Get from Where You Are to Where You Want to Be,* by Cheri Huber.

For a fun twist on money personalities, we've given them names and characters that make it easier to relate the personality with a particular way of being around money.

The main money personalities are as follows:

THE SAVER—SAMMY THE SQUIRREL

Sammy likes to save his money for things he wants to buy and for a rainy day, in case he needs money for something. He is very careful with his money; he doesn't spend it easily and finds most immediate pleasure purchases wasteful and self-indulgent.

THE SPENDER—MANNY THE MONKEY

Manny spends every cent as soon as he gets it on piddlyjunk. He often spends more money than he has and never has any money saved. He also likes to buy things and do things for friends and loves to be the life of the party. The spender is the one who often has the latest this or hottest that. Just mentioning the word "budget" makes him want to run away. Or throw up!

THE MONEY MONK—CASSIE THE CAT

Cassie doesn't feel that money is worth her time or energy. Money is beneath her. She often feels that money isn't a good thing and she just can't be bothered with it. She may feel that money isn't spiritual.

THE AVOIDER—OLIVIA THE OSTRICH

Olivia hates dealing with money. She avoids paying bills, looking at credit card statements or paying back debts. She's always in financial trouble. She doesn't know how much money she has in her wallet, exactly how much money she makes, owes or has saved—if she has any saved. She's in a perpetual 'money fog.'

THE MONEY WORRIER—CARL THE CLAM

Carl worries about money constantly. He worries about not having enough, about spending too much, about losing money on investments and about outliving his money. No matter how much money he has or doesn't have, he can't stop worrying. He is always reworking the figures in his budget just to be sure.

THE AMASSER—ANDY THE ANT

Andy wants to see his money grow constantly; saving and investing make him feel powerful and secure. He takes his laptop along on vacations to make sure his portfolio is growing every day.

You probably recognize people in your life that have one or more of these money personalities and since we're not in this world alone, you may want to learn to recognize these personality traits when you get into business and personal relationships with others.

Which money animal are you most like?   _____

Which money animal is your child most like?_____

How does your money personality show up in your life?

_____

_____

_____

_____

How does being this animal serve you?_____

_____

How does being this animal not serve you? _____

_____

And finally, just for fun, if your money personality had a bumper sticker, what would it say? _____

_____

The important thing to understand about money personalities is that they are usually run by our underlying beliefs and most often these beliefs aren't even ours!

Again, we develop beliefs from parents, teachers, family, friends, neighbors, books, magazine, movies, TV and other media. We see basic money personalities developing in the kids and teens who attend our camps. As in other areas of child development, children are usually *just like* their parents or *completely opposite* from their parents. Sometimes they rebel against one way of being only to realize later that the opposite end of the spectrum also has its drawbacks.

B T F A = R

Financial belief systems are at the core of all of our money programs and most people's financial problems. It's important to uncover and understand what drives you, and your children. These money beliefs are literally your financial foundation. If you're not consistently reaching your financial goals you may want to begin to look at and change your money beliefs, or money files, as T. Harv Eker calls them. They run your subconscious and control your choices and behaviors around money.

Let's break down one common belief about money, as an example, so you can see exactly how beliefs influence and create your life.

BELIEF: RICH PEOPLE ARE GREEDY.

Here is what happens with this belief:

Your *belief* (rich people are greedy) leads to a *thought* (I don't want to be greedy), which controls your *feelings* (discomfort at the thought of others thinking you might be greedy, and/or discomfort when you get or have money or don't make much in the first place), which leads to your *actions* (choosing to spend some or all your money), which then leads to your *result* (i.e., having little or no money left over). It looks like this:

YOUR BELIEFS lead to
YOUR THOUGHTS, which lead to
YOUR FEELINGS, which lead to
YOUR ACTIONS, which equal
YOUR RESULTS (I.E., YOUR LIFE)!

I've heard it said that if you want to know what your *real* priorities are, look at your life. You see, our beliefs influence what we really want for ourselves. I hear you saying, "But wait, I want to be out of debt!" But do you, really? Are your *actions* reflecting what you *say* you want? Remember, it's usually a subconscious belief (like a recording running in the background) that is controlling your behavior. The only way you can change your behaviors, and the results of those behaviors, is to first become *aware* of your beliefs.

Beliefs are like icebergs. It's the part of the iceberg that's beneath the surface that causes all the problems. You could also think about beliefs like this: we all know that electricity can be both a good thing or a bad thing, depending on how you use it. It's a good thing when we use it to light up our homes, make our lives easier and power the world wide web. We also know that it can cause great damage and even kill us if used the wrong way. It can be either supportive or nonsupportive of where we want to go in our lives. Financial beliefs work the same way. They're either supportive or nonsupportive; and if you want

to change your life you must first change the beliefs that are driving your life. Here is just a partial list of the most common money beliefs running people's lives:

- Rich people are greedy

- Rich people are stingy

- Having money is a huge responsibility

- People won't like me if I have a lot of money

- It's not OK to have more money than I need

- There's not enough money to go around

- I'm too stupid to have a lot of money

- I shouldn't make more money than my parents

Your kids are developing these belief recordings as we speak, so again I remind you, watch the example you're setting for them.

2ND: MAKE MONEY A FAMILY MATTER

More often than not, parents leave their children out of the family finances for one reason or another. Perhaps you have money and don't want your children to have to think about it or worry about it. Maybe you grew up in a family that never talked about money; it was a hush, hush sort of thing.

Whether you have money or not, most parents aren't comfortable with their children talking about the family's financial situation with friends, relatives and neighbors. If this is your family, then simply teach your children that talking about the family's finances is a private matter; not because it's wrong to talk about money, but simply because you'd rather they not discuss it with others.

Start by explaining to your kids that being a good person has nothing to do with how much money a person has. But you have to get to the point where *you* believe it first. The sooner we

all learn that money is simply a tool to reach our dreams, the more open we will be to discussing it and learning from each other how to use it wisely.

Parents tell us that one of the biggest reasons they don't talk to their kids about money and family finances is because they simply don't know *how* to talk to them about it. In my adult programs, parents often tell us they are embarrassed or ashamed because they haven't figured out the money thing yet. These emotions affect their ability to talk to their kids about money. They feel they can't possibly teach something they don't know. This is also one of the reasons financial literacy education is lacking in our schools. Teachers either don't have this knowledge or, if they do, they themselves aren't saving and investing. It can be very uncomfortable teaching a subject you don't know, don't understand or aren't practicing.

What should you do to involve your kids? I recommend that when your children reach about 6 years of age (earlier if they are interested), you start by showing them the household bills and letting them help you write checks, pay bills on-line, review financial statements, etc. Show them your credit card statements and the interest that's accruing if you're not paying it in full each month; this is a great place to show them how compound interest can work against you. And by all means, show them how to balance a checkbook (you do balance your checkbook, don't you?) and how to use the check register when writing checks or using your ATM card.

Teach them about getting points on credit cards. Teach them about your credit score. Go over all the utility bills so they learn to catch problems such as being overbilled or double billed or charged for things they didn't buy. Let them help you pick investment options (you have the final decision, of course) and if you have a financial advisor, invite the kids along so they can see what kinds of information you need to know in order to make wise investment decisions. Let them help you figure out your net worth (what you *own* minus what you *owe*) regularly or at least once a year.

If you're not doing these things now, hopefully the process of preparing your child will help you become better prepared, as well.

Many parents say they can't wait to discover what their kids can teach them when they come home from our camps!

If you have a family or household budget, let your child see it and help you with it. If you don't have a budget and you're one of the many people who cringe at the mere mention of the word, I'd like to invite you to re-evaluate the B-word. Instead of a budget, we call them Saving and Spending Plans, or SSPs, and they are simply another financial power tool to help you reach your dreams. We've included an SSP activity later in the book.

If you have a business, bring your child to work with you. Give her a job she can do on a regular basis. Show her the company's bills, get her involved in running the business, especially the finances. Pay her for helping you in your business (in addition to the pay in experience). This paid experience is also a great opportunity to help her open a ROTH IRA since contributions must come from earned income. There are yearly limits in regard to how much money a child can make at certain ages so make sure you consult your tax accountant about paying your child.

If you own real estate, talk to your child about getting good tenants, paying property taxes, tax rules, maintenance, and more. Walk him through the numbers as you determine the ROI (return on investment) of your properties. Let him see what it really entails to invest in real estate.

If you have one or more investment accounts in which you hold individual stocks or mutual funds, let your child help you review your monthly statements. If you can, it's also a great idea to start an account at a brokerage firm where your child can deposit his own investment money. Online accounts like TD-Ameritrade or Scott Trade are great because they generally have lower fees and are easily accessible. You'll need to open a custodial account for him (for kids under 18), and then the entire family can learn about stocks and mutual funds if you don't already understand them. Kids generally enjoy learning along with their parents, so have fun!

Bottom Line: Get them involved early so they learn that taking care of their own personal finances is just one of those things they have to do in life.

3RD: PUT YOUR CHILD IN CHARGE OF HIS OR HER OWN FINANCES

Yes, that's right. Put your child in charge of his or her own financial wants and needs, and do it sooner rather than later. Have them pay for their own things as soon as they are ready. You may be saying to yourself, "What? Give my eight-year-old hundreds of dollars and watch her go out and spend it on the things she wants?" Well, not exactly.

Aren't you spending money every day to support your child? Don't you buy him socks, pay for his soccer shoes, fund his archery lessons, buy her hair baubles, her cheer leading outfits, etc.?

Aren't you giving them money to go out with friends, go to a movie, buy a soda here and there (pop for you Midwesterners), have ice cream on special occasions, buy gifts for friends' birthdays and other such items? Yes, you are. So, here's what I'm suggesting:

Rather than spending this money *on* or *for* your child, begin running that money *THROUGH* your child instead. By doing this you will provide invaluable learning experiences around money and wealth creation, and you'll save buckets full of cash at the same time? Now doesn't that sound great? I hope so. Follow along.

Let's say you have an adorable eight-year-old daughter (aren't they all adorable?) with long hair and she loves to futz with it, braid it, put it up this way and that way and match all her outfits with hair bands, baubles and clips. Let's say that after adding it up you figure you spend about $20 a month on these assessories for her. Why not sit down with her and explain that you are now going to give her the $20 each month, divided into weekly amounts of $5 each and give her the experience of being in charge of buying her own hair supplies. How empowering would that be?

Now, take a few more things that you regularly buy for her, put them all together, divide by four and provide her with an allowance that now serves a valuable purpose. It's going to teach her how to spend, save, invest and donate her money wisely and I'll explain how this education unfolds in the next few chapters. These are only a few of the benefits of this great program.

If you still don't quite understand why letting your child be in charge of her own financial freedom is a great thing, let me ask you a question.

Remember the question I asked at the beginning of the book about preparing your child to be a great baseball player or flutist?

What *if* your child came to you and told you he wanted to grow up and become the most amazing baseball player on the face of the planet? You'd be supportive, wouldn't you?

But again, what if you never gave that child a ball to throw, catch or hit? What if you never gave that child a mitt or a bat? What if you never taught that child the rules to the game? What if you never provided the opportunity for that child to practice? What are the chances of your child growing up and becoming that great ball player? Slim to none!

This is exactly what we do to our children with regard to money.

You see, loving your child isn't enough. Our one and only goal as parents is to teach our children how to live on their own when they become adults. If we don't teach our children how to make, manage and multiply money wisely, we fail as parents. Period!

With the *Ultimate Allowance System*, your children will grow up and become pros at making, managing and multiplying their money.

NOTES:

Welcome to the Ultimate Allowance

"Maturity begins the day we accept responsibility for our own actions." —
ROBERT ALLEN, author of *Multiple Streams of Income.*

As I've suggested, you, like most parents on the face of the planet, spend money, and often lots of it, on your children. You provide shelter, food, clothes, school, medical care, and more. If you're able, you also give them money to spend on things they want as well. This money can add up to hundreds or even thousands of dollars a month, depending on your family's economic situation and the needs and desires of your children. The amount you spend can add up quickly if you allow them to 'nickel and dime' you to death, though it's probably more like 'five and tenning' you to death at this point!

The cost to raise a child from birth to age 17, according to the USDA web site, ranges from $143,000 to $289,000. In any case, that's a lot of dollars' worth of practice your child can have before he is out on his own. Doesn't it make sense to give your kids the opportunity to experience great financial triumphs as well as painful, costly mistakes with your parental guidance *before* they leave home? After all, the goal is for them to move out and stay out, right?

THE RIGHT AGE TO START

I can only speak from experience, but I wish I'd had an opportunity to learn about money when I was young.

I didn't get an allowance as a child, nor did I have much opportunity to buy things or have money in my hands. So, when I went away to college I was what I call financially oblivious. Thank goodness I didn't have to take out student loans for college because back then it was easy to qualify for grants and since I went to a state university, which wasn't expensive, I was able to graduate from college with no debt. No financial education, but at least debt-free.

67

I'm also thankful that the young man I was dating and ended up marrying (the father of my son) knew quite a bit more than I did and made very good money when he graduated (which was a couple of years before I did).

After college, I started to realize that I didn't have a clue about money. You see, it is rare that college students are required to take personal finance classes. As a result, they are now graduating with school loans and credit card debt anywhere from $2,000 to $20,000 or higher. I personally know a young woman who graduated at the top of her class with over $100,000 of debt. I ache for her. Considering all this, I believe myself to be one of the lucky ones.

In addition to the lack of financial education, back when I went to college (in the late '70s and early '80s) it wasn't as easy to get into thousands of dollars of credit card debt as it is now. But if I had known then what I know now, I would have had a completely different experience in my 20s with regard to my personal finances.

Over the years, virtually every adult I have spoken to about Money Camp for Kids or Teens (now Camp Millionaire), said the following, "I wish I had learned this information when I was young!" And then they ask, "Do you have a camp for adults?" These conversations tell me that adults everywhere wish they had been given the information and the opportunity to learn about money when they were younger.

Adults are hungry for this missing information, and it is the main reason the adult financial seminar business is so successful. There are opportunities all over the world now for adults to learn what they didn't learn when they were young. But why make kids wait until they are adults to learn about money? Creative Wealth co-created with Kidz Make Cents of Canada, its first large-scale seminar for teens and parents called *Wealth Rules! Financial Wisdom for Youth.* We created it so that kids won't have to grow up and recover from their childhoods anymore.

So, when should you get *your* kids involved with money? There are at least two schools of thought on the matter. The first school says to wait until they show an interest, kind of like sex. The second school says to do it as early as possible. My personal vote is to begin as early as possible, tempered with your knowledge of what the child is ready for or can handle.

Notice when your kids begin to show an interest in money; paying for things, counting it, asking how much things cost, asking how you spend your money, etc. Notice if they begin to get the idea of starting a little business, charging for a service, or loaning out an item or their own money and charging money (interest) for it. I've heard so many great stories over the years. I can't begin to tell you the variety of interesting, creative ideas kids come up with!

~ A Creative Wealth Coach's Story ~

"About a year ago, my daughter, who was 7 at the time, came to me completely frustrated because she wanted to make the family dinner but her Mother didn't have the time or the patience to help her do so. I saw the disappointment and desire to help in her eyes, so I quickly volunteered to help her with dinner that very night.

We went into the kitchen where she proceeded to draw up several menus with various choices of appetizers, main entrees and even desserts. She handed them out to all of the family members who made their choices and then she was off and running. I helped her in the kitchen for more than an hour while she diligently compiled all the ingredients and beautifully created plates of delicious food, made to order, for each family member.

She then called everyone in to eat and we proceeded to have a delightful time. After everyone was finished, all the while praising my daughter for her hard work and delicious creations, she slipped unnoticed into the kitchen. She returned a few minutes later with bills for everyone! The entire family was aghast! This had not been part of the deal! There had been no mention that anyone would have to ante-up for their dinner that evening.

Needless to say, since she was only 7 and we could see the entrepreneurial wheels turning inside her little being, we didn't want to miss the opportunity to lock in her lesson and effort. Dinner did cost me a bit more that evening, but it was one of the best experiences she could have had in terms of discovering ways to create financial freedom for her life.

This very incident will not only propel my daughter into her future but it also got me thinking about how I could help encourage kids all over the UK to think as she had. I went to the internet, typed a few keywords into Google and there was The Money Camp (now Creative Wealth International). I'm happy to say that after attending their incredible, life-changing Train the Trainer *program, I am in the process of setting up Money Camp programs in the UK!"* ~ TAYO, MONEY INSIGHTS, UK

Usually children begin to show interest in money between six and eight years of age. Sometimes a child may show absolutely no interest in money at all. Maybe he doesn't want a bunch of things. Maybe he reads a lot or plays a sport, or for whatever reason, he just doesn't show any interest. In this case, if you don't notice any natural interest by age eight or nine, start the program anyway. He may be very accepting of it even though he hasn't shown any external interest.

Occasionally, you will have a child who just flat out doesn't want anything to do with money. Often this child doesn't want the responsibility and, in this case, you need to ask yourself, "What has my child seen, heard or experienced about money that would make him feel this way?" Most likely, but not always, something has happened that caused him to associate money with something negative or painful and he just doesn't want anything to do with it. Or he may not want anything to do with it for no apparent reason at all. In either case, simply show the child the 'why' behind what you're doing.

YOUR MONEY JARS

Before we get to the actual 'how-tos,' I want to introduce you to another of our favorite financial power tools — The Money Jars.

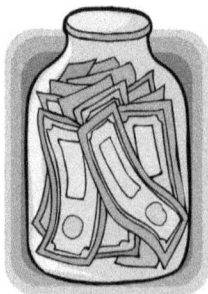

The Money Jars is a simple method of allocating your money into six different categories so that you always have money for everything you need and want.

I learned about this wonderful money management system many years ago at a seminar called *The Millionaire Mind Intensive,* a life-changing program produced by Peak Potentials. Adults who attend my programs that this system alone changes their finanical lives forever. For more information, visit:

www.peakpotentials.com/a/tofreedomandbeyond

Using the Ultimate Allowance along with the Money Jars will give your kids a powerful learning environment that will follow them into adulthood. Used correctly and regularly, the Money Jars will lead them to financial success, especially if they've gone through a financial education program like *Camp Millionaire, Money Camp, Wealth Rules* or any number of other financial programs. With that in mind, let me introduce you to your new friends, the Money Jars.

SAVE YOURSELF TIME ENERGY & MONEY

Have you ever been to McDonald's? Have you noticed that a Big Mac in San Francisco tastes pretty much the same as a Big Mac in New York? Why? How have they been able to assure that the taste, presentation and quality are always the same, no matter where you purchase the product?

It's because McDonald's has developed a *system* that works. An acronym for SYSTEM I found recently is Save YourSelf Time Energy and Money. The Money Jars is a financial system that will do just that *if* you use it on a regular basis. Let's explore how they work.

Have you ever heard yourself, or someone else, say, "I know I need to start saving money, I just don't have any money LEFT OVER." Or, "If I have any money LEFT OVER, then I'll save it"?

The Money Jars make sure that you never have more month left over at the end of your money. Since this situation normally occurs because there is no planning and no system in place, your Jars ensure that there IS money for saving, investing and more.

Before we begin, I'd like to suggest that money is simply a tool to help you reach your dreams (just like a budget). I'd also like to suggest that your money doesn't have just one job (spending); it has several different jobs. One survey estimated that *three out of every four* Americans (that's 75%) live month to month. In other words, they live paycheck to paycheck, meaning they spend every cent they make every month and don't save or invest at all. In addition, we've also read that for every $1.00 Americans do make, they spend $1.10 or more, which means they are using credit (other people's money) in the form of credit cards and balance transfers, as well as spending their savings or investment money. In addition, for the past couple of years, America has had a negative savings rate! We are spending more money than we are earning, which is *not* the way to become financially free!

CREATIVE WEALTH PRINCIPLE
It's Better to Tell Your Money Where to Go Than to Ask it Where it Went.

Have you ever said, "I wish I could do this," or "I wish I could go there," or "I wish I could take that class," or "I wish I could go on that vacation, but I just can't afford it?" If you're like most people, you say these things quite regularly. As a person who teaches basic financial skills, I hear people talking all the time and I have to admit, most of the conversation revolves around money in some way or another. It's just on peoples' minds.

What if I could show you and your family a system to manage your money—a money *habit*—that's as easy as counting to six? What if this system made it so that you always had the money to do the things you want and need to do? Would you be interested? Great! Let me show you the system.

Money Jars are a way to allocate your money so that it can serve many different functions in your life. It doesn't matter whether you have $1 to divide or $1000, the most important aspect of the Money Jars system is that it helps you develop a great money habit that will lead you toward becoming financially free. And since human beings are creatures of habit, the earlier you teach your kids about the Money Jars, the better.

Kids in our program love the Money Jars. They come back to camp the day after we've introduced the Money Jars with their own sets of jars. They are excited and proud to have their own jars.

There are six basic Money Jars:

Living • Freedom • Savings • Education • Play • Donation

All Your Income

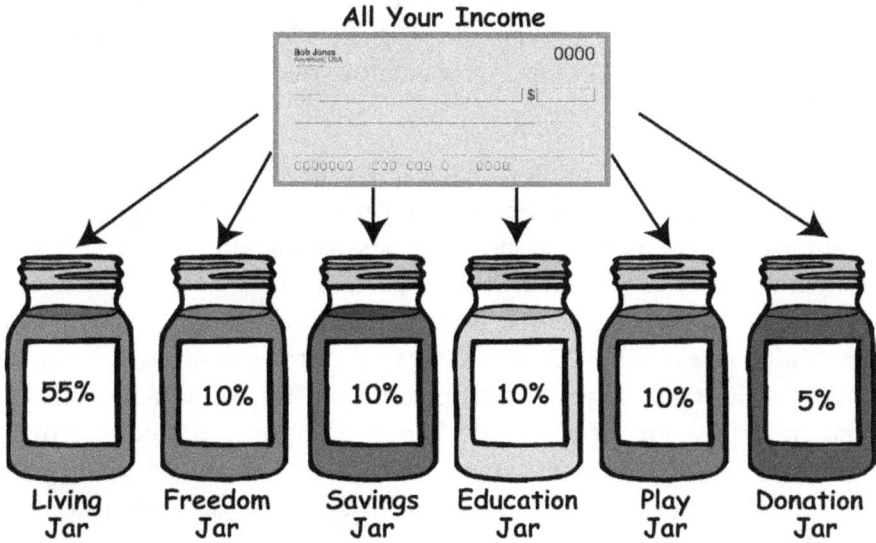

Living Jar	Freedom Jar	Savings Jar	Education Jar	Play Jar	Donation Jar
55%	10%	10%	10%	10%	5%

And they work this way:

Take *all* of your income, regardless of the source, and divide it up into six different jars or accounts. The only exception is money you didn't know you were getting (birthday money, bonuses, gifts). We suggest you put this money directly into your Freedom account.

NOTE: The percentages listed are for adults. The kids' percentages will be different at first and I'll show you how to figure them later.

YOUR LIVING JAR is for living expenses; the things you need to live each month, like housing, food, clothing, insurance, etc. This jar is normally a checking account for adults. For kids, it can be a jar or a bank account with a debit card if they are older and ready for this responsibility. If they are young, a jar is fine.

55% GOES INTO YOUR LIVING JAR.

YOUR FREEDOM JAR is your Financial Freedom Account. This money is what you invest regularly to grow so that you have money in the future. Think of this jar as your Golden Goose (see the story on page 191); every year it's going to produce enough income (golden eggs) for you to live on when you stop working. This money will be invested so that it makes more money for you; it's money you put to work for you.

Use your FREEDOM money to invest in (purchase) assets like stocks, real estate, business and other investments that will appreciate in value over time, as well as produce passive income. Passive income is income you don't trade your time and energy for, so you can eventually work because you want to, not because you have to. For an adult, your FREEDOM money may go into your 401K account at work (or a 403(b) if you work for a nonprofit), your IRA accounts and other investment accounts. It may also be in a stock account that you manage or is managed for you by a financial advisor or broker. We'll talk later about what your child can do with his or her FREEDOM Jar money.

10% GOES INTO YOUR FREEDOM JAR

Showing your child how money grows over time is critically important. This concept is often referred to as the *time value* of money. Kids are no different than we are (adults, that is) when it comes to convincing them to start a new habit or learn new information; there must be a 'why' that makes sense to them. You must tell them WIIFT (what's in it for them).

The concept of compound interest or compound growth is often challenging for a young child. A great way to show a young child how compound interest works is by using M&Ms or marbles or something else they are interested in; it's a great visual that allows them to begin seeing how their money can make more money. For a teen, it's great to use an actual bank statement to get this point across. For any age, use the Magic of Compound Growth activity on page 128.

Compound growth is an important concept to understand when it comes to investing. Make sure your child gets it! See page 180 for a chart on how a dollar grows over time.

NOTE: Girls and women should put 12-15% in their FREEDOM jar. Women have an average of fourteen fewer years of earning power because they are often taking care of children on one end of their lives and elderly parents on the other end. Women, on average, also end up divorced twice, raising the kids alone. Finally, because women live longer on average than men, they must prepare for it financially by investing a higher percentage of their earnings. The extra money is usually taken from the LIVING jar.

YOUR SAVINGS JAR has two purposes. First, it is contingency money; also called your rainy day or 'just in case' money. Imagine having three to six months' worth of living expenses put away 'just in case.' (This figure is commonly suggested by financial advisors.) If you ever lose your job or are injured, for example, you can take more time to think about where you want to your life to go. For an adult, this money needs to be easily accessible, or liquid.

Second, this jar is the one in which you save up for a larger purchase, like a car or a vacation or new computer. You can divide this part of the jar into several smaller jars depending on what you're saving for.

10% GOES INTO YOUR SAVINGS JAR

YOUR EDUCATION JAR is for learning new things. Wouldn't it be great if you always had money to learn new things?

"Education is nine-tenths of any battle."
~ NAPOLEON BONAPARTE

Most adults want to continue their education after they are out of school or graduate from college. With your education jar, there's always money to take a class or attend a seminar. For kids, this jar can be money for college or lessons.

♪ **NOTE:** The money you use to pay for your child's education is part of *your* LIVING Jar.

10% GOES INTO YOUR EDUCATION JAR

YOUR PLAY JAR is for just what it says: PLAY! There's a reason Play rhymes with Yay! This jar is for doing anything you wish that makes you happy and brings you pleasure. It's money to blow on anything you really want to have or want to do. You are required to spend it *every* month or at least every three months if you're saving up for something big. Just imagine...your child will have her own money to buy that new computer game or doll she wants so badly, and you can have that massage once a month or order a nice bottle of wine with dinner if you desire.

Most people work hard for their money, but never take time to spend this money for pleasure without feeling guilty about it. Your Play Jar gives you a way to always have money to simply blow any way you wish, and remember, it's *guilt-free*. I'm always amazed by the number of adults who ask me if spending their PLAY money is mandatory. The answer is YES! What happens when you hold onto something too tightly? It either breaks or it slips out of your hands. Money works the same way. So, go and enjoy it, but only spend the money in your Play Jar. That's what it's for!

10% GOES INTO YOUR PLAY JAR

YOUR DONATION JAR is for giving back and doing good in the world. Almost everyone I talk to says that doing things for others makes them feel good. Now you have a way to help others on a regular basis.

The donation aspect of your financial habits tells the world how you view the supply of money, and everything else, coming into your life. What if you believe there isn't enough money in the world for everyone? Do you think you would feel comfortable donating some of your money to help others? Probably not. This type of belief is referred to as a scarcity mind-set.

If, however, you believe there is an abundance of wealth in the world, you'd probably feel great about giving your time, energy and money to others. By the way, when I talk about wealth I'm talking about a wealth of anything — friends, relationships, experiences, happiness, health. The word *wealth* refers to an abundance of something.

Even though our focus here is financial freedom, and learning the financial rules that we all need to win the money game as we call it, it's not the only thing we should be teaching our kids.

There is a Universal Law that works like this: if you give something away, it comes back to you multiplied. I have learned that it isn't necessarily important that you understand exactly *how* something works to know that it *does* work. This is my own experience with the Law of Abundance. Every time I have chosen to give of myself (donate my time, energy or money), within days it was returned in one form or another. It just works and it has to do with our beliefs about abundance. For an excellent discussion on the Law of Abundance, read *The Abundance Book*, by John Randolf Price.

Again, how willing you are to spend the money in your DONATION Jar is a reflection of whether or not you think there's enough money to go around. Many adults hold the belief that because everyone else has money, there's not enough for them. It's not a zero-sum game (which means that there is a finite amount of money, or anything, for that matter, in the world) and when one person gains a dollar, another loses a dollar. It doesn't work that way. The amount of value that can be created in the world is limitless; it's limited only by your creativity, ability and desire to make things happen in your life.

Think of your DONATION Jar in terms of doing something nice for someone, for example, smiling at a stranger or complimenting someone's appearance. The movie, *Pay It Forward,* is the perfect example of this idea. Positive energy gets transferred from you to another person, and then keeps getting transferred to others until it's finally returned back to you in some form, usually multiplied.

Remember, however, that *like attracts like*, so if you give away your time, you'll probably get time back. If you give away your money, you'll probably get money back; from my own experience, life most often seems to work this way.

NOTE: It's important not to give money away just to get money back in return, but give it away because it's the right thing to do and it makes you and others feel good.

Recently, I was in a coffee shop, working on this book, actually, and I was watching a couple with a teen-age boy in tow. They were very disturbed; it was obvious that something was wrong in their world. As they left, I quickly purchased a great big, yummy chocolate chip cookie, ran out the door and gave it to the young man, just because. They all smiled, told me their car wasn't working and they were stranded and that the cookie was the nicest thing that had happened in a while. It was just a simple act, yet it made a world of difference for a family that had forgotten the simple joys of just being together during what they would later recall as just a little crisis.

Be mindful of how your money beliefs show up, and remember, your children are watching.

5% GOES INTO YOUR DONATION JAR

NOTE: If you normally tithe or donate 10% each month, then it is suggested that you take the extra 5% from your Living Jar. The word 'tithe' by the way, literally means 1/10. For more information about the Money Jars, visit:

www.creativewealthintl.org/moneyjars.php

Now that you understand the basic Money Jar principles, let me answer a few common questions about them before I finally introduce you to the Ultimate Allowance System.

Q. DO YOU HAVE TO USE ACTUAL JARS? GLASS OR PLASTIC?

No, you can use any kind of container you wish; however, it is important that the jars or containers be clear (see-through). The visual accumulation of money is critical in a child's ever-expanding world of money and its meaning in the world. As she puts money into the jars, and watches it accumulate, she is encouraged to add to the jars even more.

As adults, we're encouraged when we look at our bank and investment statements each month. Don't you get excited when you see your investments growing month by month? If you haven't started saving and investing yet, now is a great time to start, right along with your child. You will enjoy seeing your money grow, too! Believe it or not, your child won't be disappointed, embarrassed or upset that you're just starting out. It's us who have these emotions. Your child would love to do this with you and have you to celebrate with as you both learn together how to save and invest over time.

Q. WHAT ELSE COULD WE USE AS JARS?

We've seen kids use Zip-Lock bags, plastic peanut butter containers and more. Kids are creative and have fun labeling and decorating their jars. It's a great family activity. Just make room on that dining room table, put on some music, gather markers, tape, paper and any other art supplies you have around the house and have at it.

Q. WHAT IF MY CHILD IS AFRAID THAT SOMEONE MAY TAKE THE MONEY OUT OF HIS JARS?

If your child is fearful of losing his money, it's an issue that should be addressed immediately. The fear that he may lose the money once he saves it is very unhealthy. A child who develops this emotion about money or has an experience where his money is taken or stolen by another, may grow into an adult who doesn't trust others when it comes to money, or maybe anything else in life, for that matter.

Children shouldn't have to live in fear of anything, so ask yourself, why is my child afraid? Deal with whatever comes up as soon as possible to help the child overcome his fear of loss. Then figure out what you can do to ensure that the child's room, and his money, are safe and secure. As a last resort, get the child a small safe or something with a lock, or better yet, start his first saving's account at a bank close by so it's easy for him to deposit his money on a regular basis.

Q. WHAT IF MY CHILD IS OLDER AND DOESN'T WANT TO KEEP JARS IN HIS ROOM? ARE THERE OTHER OPTIONS FOR OLDER KIDS AND TEENS?

If you have a child or teen who is computer savvy, first make sure that he has at least one, and preferably two, bank accounts; a checking and a savings. Make sure they are accounts with no fees. Then set him up using a spreadsheet in which he inputs the amount of money he is receiving, $100 for example, and then transfers the amount into 6 or more columns (depending on how many things he is saving up for) that represent each jar.

You can set this spreadsheet up to automatically tally the totals as he adds and subtracts money to and from his jar accounts. Another idea is to set up the spreadsheet to automatically divide the money into the jars, or columns, using simple calculations based on percentages you put in the program. A simple version might look like this:

Date	Amount	Memo	Living	Freedom	Saving	School	Play	Give
6/2/07	100.00	Paycheck	55.00	10.00	10.00	10.00	10.00	5.00
Balance			55.00	10.00	10.00	10.00	10.00	5.00
6/15/07	25.00	Gift	13.75	2.50	2.50	2.50	2.50	1.25
Balance	125.00		68.75	12.50	12.50	12.50	12.50	6.25

When he wants to "spend" his jar money, he simply takes the money out of the appropriate bank account (jar) and makes an adjustment in the jar column. You can also keep track of these accounts by hand, using this spreadsheet and a calculator. For a copy of a blank spreadsheet you can begin with, download one here:

www.ultimateallowancebook.com/UAB/spreadsheetjars.xls

Q. DOES THIS PROGRAM WORK FOR ADULTS?

ABSOLUTELY! Not only is this system taught to hundreds of thousands of adults each year at Peak Potential's *Millionaire Mind Intensive*, it is also the system we teach in our *Camp Millionaire*,

Moving Out! and *Creative Wealth Intensive for Adults* and *Women*. It is a powerful, effective method for allocating your money…if you do it.

Q. DO ADULTS HAVE ACTUAL JARS OR SIX BANK ACCOUNTS?

Most adults have separate checking and savings accounts, in a bank or credit union, that represent each jar, with the exception of their FREEDOM account. This account is often represented by several different types of investment accounts.

For instance, you might have a portion of your FREEDOM money going into a 401K account at work and part in an investment account with a brokerage company (TD-Ameritrade, Ameriprise, ING Direct, Morgan Stanley, Charles Schwab, etc.). You might also have an account in which you are saving your FREEDOM money to purchase real estate, start a business or buy stocks or mutual funds on your own. For a simple example of how one of our coaches set up her jars, download this file:

www.creativewealthintl.org/downloads/UAB/INGJars.pdf

Also, a great jar to keep in your home is the classic SPARE CHANGE JAR. You can keep one of these jars individually or as a family. Start the simple habit of putting all of your change from your pockets or wallet in this jar each evening. You'll be surprised at how quickly it adds up. Sometimes I save it up for vacation and sometimes I put it in my FREEDOM account. It feels great when you roll up all your change and find you have $100 you didn't know you had! This activity is a also a great one to do with your kids.

Q. DO COUPLES NEED SEPARATE SETS OF JARS OR ACCOUNTS?

Preferably. We think it's a great idea for each person to have his or her own money to allocate and spend. Differences in money beliefs, philosophies and habits are a major cause of divorce and stress in relationships. Issues around money can cause resentments and eventually destroy an otherwise perfect union.

By having separate sets of jars or accounts, both parties are responsible for their own finances. Both people feel empowered because they have their own money to manage without having to get 'approval' from the other. There are many ways to implement this system, so have a talk with your spouse or partner to develop a method that works for both of you. Some couples have their own jars, and also have a joint set for the family.

And don't neglect that PLAY Jar. It's important that both parties have the same amount to play with, otherwise resentments can develop and wreak havoc with the relationship.

Hopefully, you can now see why I have incorporated the powerful Money Jar system into the Ultimate Allowance. Combined, they will help lead to your children's financial success later in life.

HOW THE JARS WORK

Let's talk in adult terms first. If the net amount (after taxes) of your monthly paycheck is $3000, you would allocate this money as follows:

MONEY JAR	PERCENTAGE	$3000 DOLLARS
Living Jar	55%	$1650
FREEDOM Jar	10%	$300
Saving Jar	10%	$300
Education Jar	10%	$300
Play Jar	10%	$300
Donation Jar	10%	$150

Even if you have money taken out of your paycheck for a 401K or other tax-deferred retirement program, it's a great idea to allocate another 10% to another FREEDOM account, if you can. If you can't, then simply divide your paycheck into the other five jars. If you can put extra into your FREEDOM account, just imagine how much faster you're going to be free!

So what happens when you get extra money, like a bonus check or company profit sharing? You can either divide the money into all the jars or put it all into your FREEDOM account to invest as you wish. If, for example, you got a holiday bonus check for $750, the two methods would look like this:

MONEY JAR	PERCENTAGE	$750 DOLLARS
Living Jar	55%	$412.50 *or* $0
FREEDOM Jar	10%	$75 *or* $750
Saving Jar	10%	$75 *or* $0
Education Jar	10%	$75 *or* $0
Play Jar	10%	$75 *or* $0
Donation Jar	5%	$37.50 *or* $0

Let's say your daughter gets $100 cash as a birthday gift from her favorite aunt (like your bonus at work). You can have her allocate this extra money as follows:

MONEY JAR	PERCENTAGE	$100 DOLLARS
Living Jar	55%	$55
FREEDOM Jar	10%	$10
Saving Jar	10%	$10
Education Jar	10%	$10
Play Jar	10%	$10
Donation Jar	5%	$5

Once this habit is established, you and your kids will start noticing how the money in each jar, or account, is accumulating and growing. This 'visual accumulation' is a great motivator to continue using your jars. I can only speak from experience, but when I see my investments growing each month, I get very excited! That's what I hope happens with you and your kids!

What about percentages for kids? Well, at first, aside from gifts or bonuses mentioned above, the amounts that are going into each jar will be very different than the target percentages for adults. As you begin to understand more about how the program works, you'll see that in the beginning, we're just making sure they are using the jar system fully. As they get older and become responsible for more and more of their own financial needs, the percentages will slowly come into alignment with the adult percentages. Until then, just remember that the goal is to establish great habits first. The details and refinement of the jar system will come later.

LET'S TALK ABOUT NEEDS AND WANTS

Hopefully, the jar system seems pretty simple so far, but before we move on, we want your son or daughter to understand the difference between a NEED and a WANT.

If you look at the worksheet on page 89 with the list of items we use as an example, you'll notice a W or an N in the right column next to each item. We've labeled the items *needs* or *wants* in the way we think they probably should be categorized, although your child may do his best to convince you that the Nintendo game he *wants* is a need because it helps improve his coordination!

Talking about the family finances in terms of *needs* versus *wants* lets you help your child understand how much it actually costs to raise a family and run a household. Use the following chart to talk with him about things that you consider needs versus wants.

Although distinguishing a need from a want is pretty straightforward, the area of transportation is always subjective. Our view is that transportation is a need; a car is a want. Teens often get very excited about saving up for their first car. However, when you show them what that car will actually cost in payments, gas, insurance and maintenance, they may decide to forgo the car until they have their first steady job.

Use the following simple chart with your child to explore the difference between needs and wants. Ask him what he considers to be needs and what he considers to be wants. If he suggests something is a need when it is actually a want, gently explain why you think it's not a need.

You may be surprised later on when your child tells you he really doesn't want or need something. You'll be *really* surprised when he tells you that what you're buying is a want, and that you shouldn't be buying it because you don't need it!

NEEDS	WANTS

Now that you've done this activity with your child, he should have a good sense for what is a need and what is a want. You and your child should be very clear on this concept in order to allocate the allowance items to the appropriate jars when you get to the worksheets coming up.

WHAT IT COSTS TO RAISE ME

On page 87-88, you'll see one of the most valuable Wealth Work[2] assignments we give kids and teens during our Camp Millionaire and Moving Out! programs. It's called, *What It Costs to Raise Me.*

Both kids and teens come back the day after this assignment is given and are flabbergasted at how much it actually costs their parents to raise them! They constantly tell us they had no idea how 'spoiled' they were, and we've noticed it doesn't matter what socioeconomic level they come from, (i.e., how much money their parents have). They all say the same thing. Parents tell us how much they appreciate doing this activity with their kids as it often makes the kids think before asking their parents for something.

---

2 Wealthy people do wealthwork at night, not homework; for example, they research stocks, write business plans, look for real estate deals in the paper or on the internet, etc.

Please take time to do this activity with your child before you introduce him to the allowance program. The activity is designed for the child to do, so just hand him the page and let him do it. Help out if you need, though. You'll be glad you did.

NOTES:

WHAT IT COSTS TO RAISE ME

Do you have any idea what your parents will spend to raise you from birth to age 17? Probably not.

According to the U.S. Department of Agriculture, it costs between **$150,000** and **$290,000** to raise a child from birth to 17! Maybe this will cause you to think twice before begging your parents for things.

Fill in your guess in the first column and then ask your parent(s) for the real answer!

How much do you think your family spends per year for...

EXPENSE	YOUR GUESS	REALITY
Housing		
Food		
Clothing		
Health care		
Childcare		
Education		
Transportation		
Extra-curricular activities		
Vacations		

NOW, LET'S LOOK AT SOME OF THE MISCELLANEOUS THINGS YOUR PARENTS BUY FOR YOU:

1. My newest pair of sneakers or shoes cost _____.

2. It cost _____ to have my teeth cleaned this year.

3. I get _____ for lunch or snack money each week.

4. The last time I went to a movie it cost _____.

5. My last sport/music lesson cost my parents _____.

6. My newest piece of clothing cost _____.

7. What does it cost your parents to take you to the doctor? _____

8. What was your share of the last family vacation? _____

9. What did it cost your parents this year for birthday and Christmas presents? _____

10. How much money are your parents putting away every month for your college education? _____

11. What did it cost last time you got your hair cut? _____

12. What did it cost your parents the last time you went to a friend's birthday party? _____

ARE YOU SHOCKED?

_____ A LITTLE OR _____ A LOT

Ultimate Allowance How-tos

Let's get back to our little 8-year-old girl with the hair baubles. You were spending about $20 a month on hair accessories for her.

In our worksheet below, let's add the other things you pay for, to see how much you spend on her each month. Decide if the item is a need or a want and note that in the last column.

WORKSHEET A—STEP I

ITEM	COST PER MONTH	WANT OR NEED
Hair accessories	$20	W
Movie rentals	$20	W
Clothes	$75	N
Shoes	$30	N
Books	$20	W or N
School Supplies	$10	N
Gifts for friends	$15	W
Doll Supplies	$10	W
Candy, etc.	$10	W
Soccer supplies	$30	W or N
Dance lessons	$200	W or N
MONTHLY TOTAL	**$440**	

Before we take the Money Jars into consideration, if we simply ran the money we're currently spending on her *through* her, her allowance would look like this:

$440 a month *or*

$220 twice a month *or*

$110 week

ADDING THE MONEY JARS TO THE EQUATION

You're now going to *pad* her allowance so that she has enough money to use her Money Jars and begin developing her first great financial habit. Let's revisit the percentages that we used, remembering they are adult percentages and are used only as a guide. They can and should be modified to fit your family's individual financial situation. When setting up the system for yourself, don't modify the percentages too much or they won't be the powerful financial management tool they are intended to be.

Living Jar	55%	
FREEDOM Jar	10%	(12% for girls)
Saving Jar	10%	
Education Jar	10%	
Play Jar	10%	
Donation Jar	5%	

When parents first learn about the Money Jar system, they often ask why kids need a Living Jar, because, after all, they are usually footing the bill for their kids' living expenses. Using the money you are already spending for living expenses is the whole point. By having your child manage the money for his own needs, or running this money *through* your child instead, guess who gets to practice? Exactly...your kids! And remember, practice makes _____?

But what about the idea that you are funding her saving and investing jars? Well, what about it? Remember, we're instilling habits, beliefs, principles and more with this system. After your child gets started, you may find that she naturally wants to earn money of her own, which is a good thing. I want you to encourage your kids from the very beginning to start thinking of ways they can bring money into their lives. As they begin to make money, you can deal with it in several ways. We'll go over this later. For now, just understand that you will be helping to fund her Money Jars initially.

Let's talk about the BIG living expenses like rent, food, school tuition, insurance; things like that. These expenses aren't normally something that you would ever run through your child. It just doesn't make sense. The payments are large; and well, it's just a parent sort of thing to have to pay. Show your kids the bills and teach them about these expenses, of course, but don't worry about running these expenses through your kids.

Now, here's another scenario. Let's say your whole family gets together to plan your next vacation. The kids all agree that in order to help you fund it, they won't ask to go out to dinner, they will check out books and videos from the local library and they will do odd jobs for neighbors and friends in order to have spending money while on vacation. Let's say that two of your three children save $100 each. Your third child, however, only saves $25. What do you do in this case? Is it fair that the third child only has a quarter of what the other two have to spend? This is a very interesting question.

Did all three children agree to earn and save their own money to spend? Did all three have the same opportunities to be creative, energetic, motivated? Was the child who came up short, physically and emotionally capable of earning as much money as the others? If the answer to these questions is Yes, then my suggestion is that the third child simply has $25 to spend. It is a valuable lesson for that child. It's also a great opportunity for the other kids to help out if they choose by lending or giving their brother or sister additional money to spend on the vacation. Helping shouldn't be mandatory though, as it would defeat the purpose. Helping should always be something they WANT to do. This is a great place to use their Donation Jar money. Again, only if they choose to help out.

The key is to decide, up front, how much YOU are willing to provide them and how much THEY are expected to earn and save on their own. If some of your children are a lot younger than others, then work out a system during the family planning meeting in which you all agree how much each person will contribute to the vacation or special event. All in all, it's about making and keeping agreements. Children are never too young to learn how important it is to keep their word to others, and especially to themselves.

There will be times when you must be strong in your intention to let your children learn by experience. In the example above, if you cave in and give the third child money, you will be doing a disservice to that child, and his siblings, and again, setting up beliefs that may include always expecting others to rescue him if he doesn't do his share. Just remember to ask yourself this question, "What am I teaching my child right now with my choices and behaviors?"

Back to our 8-year-old. Using Worksheet A—Step II below, let's look at our example list again. We've determined which jar or jars the expense money would come out of (once it gets in there in the first place) and written the jar name in the right column.

Though most of the items are fairly straightforward, you'll notice that there are two items that could be allocated into a couple of different jars. It's really your child's decision, with your guidance, of course.

Worksheet A—Step II

Item	Cost	Money Jar
Hair accessories	$20	Play Jar
Movie rentals	$20	Play Jar
Clothes	$75	Living Jar
Shoes	$30	Living Jar
Books	$20	Education or Play Jar
School supplies	$10	Education Jar
Gifts for friends	$15	Living Jar
Doll supplies	$10	Play Jar
Candy, etc.	$10	Play Jar
Soccer supplies	$30	Play Jar
Dance lessons	$200	Education or Play Jar
TOTAL	$440	

Next, add up each jar column (L, F, S, E, P, D) on the Example Worksheet A on page 95. You'll see that Parts I and II are now combined into one Worksheet A. Put the total for each jar in the bottom row. Now circle the percentages related to the Jars used in the list above. In this case, the Living, Education and Play Jars.

If you look on page 95, you'll see that you are now going to transfer these jar totals that you just circled in Worksheet A (bottom row) into Worksheet B (first column). What we're about to do now may seem a little complicated, at first. However, the steps are laid out in a very simple progression. Give yourself permission to be confused at first and know once you get it, it will make sense. It IS worth the effort, I promise.

Just follow the instructions for Worksheets A and B on the next page. Go slowly step by step and I guarantee you'll find your way to a very solid plan designed with your child's future financial success in mind.

We'll be working on our original example and then you'll use your own blank forms to figure out your own child's Ultimate Allowance.

WORKSHEET A AND B INSTRUCTIONS

These are the steps. After following along with the example, use these same steps to figure out your own child's allowance on the blank forms on page 104 and 105. In our example, Worksheet A was divided into Part I and Part II before it was combined so that you could see what we're doing. In the worksheet you'll be using, the two parts are combined into one Worksheet A.

WORKSHEET A—EXAMPLE (PG 95), BLANK TEMPLATE (PG 104)

1. Figure out how much you spend on your child each month by listing the items, their average cost and then labeling each item as a need or a want.

2. Determine which jar each item belongs to and put the amount from #1 in the corresponding jar column.

3. Add up each column and put the total jar amount in the bottom row across from JAR TOTALS. (In this case, I'm referring to the 120, 230 and 90.)

4. Circle the jar columns that contain any amount of money (120, 230, 90).

5. Add the column totals and put that total in the box to the right of the equal sign (in this case, $440).

WORKSHEET B—EXAMPLE (PG 95), BLANK TEMPLATE (PG 105).

1. Transfer the Jar Totals you circled in #4 above to Worksheet B under TOTAL PER JAR and circle them again (120, 230, 90).

2. Transfer Total Spent (#5 above) down to Jar Totals.

2. Circle the corresponding percentages under ADULT JAR %.

3. Add up the JAR % and put in bottom row, right most column (the 75%).

4. Use the explanation starting on page 97 to determine how much you need to pad your child's allowance with to provide him enough money to use his Money Jars correctly.

5. Determine if you will give out his allowance weekly, bi-weekly or monthly.

Example Worksheet A

Item or Activity	Cost per month of each jar						Want/ Need
	L	F	S	E	P	D	
Hair accessories					20		W N
Movie rentals					20		W N
Clothes	75						W N
Shoes	30						W N
Books				20			W N
School Supplies				10			W N
Gifts for friends	15						W N
Doll supplies					10		W N
Candy, etc.					10		W N
Soccer supplies					30		W N
Dance lessons				200			W N
JAR TOTALS	120	0	0	230	90	0	= $440

*JARS: L=Living, F=Financial Freedom Account, S=Savings, E=Education, P=Play, D=Donation

Example Worksheet B

MONEY JAR	TOTAL PER JAR	ADULT JAR %
Living Jar	$120	55%
FFA Jar	0	10%
Savings Jar	0	10%
Education Jar	$230	10%
Play Jar	$90	10%
Donation Jar	0	5%
JAR TOTALS	$440	75%

INTRODUCE THE SYSTEM TO YOUR CHILD, COMPLETE AND SIGN BOTH AGREEMENTS.

1. Have your child create his own set of Money Jars (or take him to the bank to open his own accounts).

2. Show your child how to create an SSP (budget) in order to be able to plan his saving and spending.

3. Help guide your child through the weeks, months and years that follow with continual education and encouragement as he learns through making wise and not-so-wise choices.

4. Re-evaluate the program every three to six months until he moves out and is successfully in charge of his life!

5. Have a glass of champagne (or sparkling cider), pat yourself on the back and know you did a very good thing.

"Yeah! We did it!"

OK, let's continue. The instructions are listed sequentially beginning back on page 96 so please refer back to them at any time if you get lost or confused. Again, I promise it's worth the effort.

You're going to need a calculator soon so make sure you have one handy.

Add up the percentages for all the jars that were used in the calculations on page 97 on Example Worksheet B. In other words, if the items you are paying for listed on Worksheet A come from the Living Jar, the Education Jar and the Play Jar, add up the percentages for those jars based on the adult guidelines.

The jar percentages add up like this:

Living Jar + Education Jar + Play Jar or...

$$55\% + 10\% + 10\% = 75\%$$

Have you got that calculator handy? Great. The final step is to determine the total amount of the allowance you're going to give your child.

In our example, we've already figured out that the total amount we spend on our 8-year old daughter is $440 a month. Since we've used three of the Money Jars already, we're going to say that $440 is equal to 75% of the total you need to provide to your child so that she can use her Money Jars correctly.

Here is the math you'll use to figure the grand total you need to provide your child as her Ultimate Allowance:

$$440 \text{ divided by } 75\% \text{ (.75) or } 440/.75 = \$587$$

IMPORTANT REMINDER: The final allowance amounts given for each jar will NOT match the percentages that are initially given for the adult system. The goal is to eventually teach the child to be able to divide his income into these percentages, but at first, they will be skewed. We use the calculation above simply to give the child money to put in the jars that aren't being used, based on the items she'll be paying for initially.

Gradually, as the child gets closer and closer to moving out and being on her own, following the original percentages will become more important so that she learns to use the system as an adult.

The next step is to decide, based on your child, how often you will dole out her allowance. Weekly is good for ages 6-10, every other week is good for 10-13 and monthly might be a great new challenge for over 13. These are only guidelines, though, and it helps to look at what the expenses actually are. If some of the allowance includes weekly costs, like lessons, it might be wise to give it out weekly. If not, every other week or on the first of the month might work well. If you try one way and you think your child would handle it better another way, change it. There's no cut-and-dried way of allocating the allowance. Every child is different, so a little trial and error is perfectly fine.

It's best to discuss with your child how often you will provide the allowance, and come to an agreement about it together. Have an understanding right away that if it doesn't work one way, you can always re-evaluate and do it another way. Always keep in mind that this is your child's program and you want him to feel empowered, so make sure to include him in every step and every decision.

So, continuing on with our example . . . your daughter's allowance has been figured at $587 per month. This translates to:

$147 per week, or

$294 every other week, or

$587 on the first of the month.

At this point, I suspect you are thinking to yourself (or even saying out loud), "Whoa, that's a whole lot of money to give an 8-year-old!" Well, is it? After all, aren't you spending a lot of that money 'on' her already? Isn't it worth the extra $147 a month ($587 minus $440) to help her establish a habit that may set her up for a lifetime of financial success?

Keep in mind that she won't be spending this money all by herself. You will be guiding her every step of the way. This is why it's so critical that you make a commitment to doing whatever it takes. It's going to take your time and attention to create this financially responsible adult.

Remember that the extra money is going into her remaining three money jars:

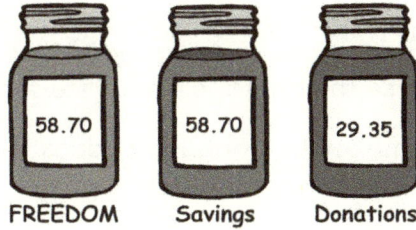

FREEDOM · Savings · Donations

Freedom ($59)   Savings ($59)   Donation ($29)

You can round the numbers up or down if you wish. It doesn't matter either way. It's the principles that are important here.

Based on $587 per month, the final accounting of her allowance broken down into her jars is as follows.

Money Jar	% of Total (roughly)	Amount
Living	22	$120.00
FREEDOM	10	$59.00
Saving	10	$59.00
Education	37	$230.00
Play	15	$90.00
Donation	5	$30.00
TOTAL	**99**	**$588.00**

When you look at it this way, it doesn't seem like that much money. Just look at the habits and belief system you're setting her up to learn:

- **She'll feel empowered when she learns to be responsible for paying for her own needs and wants.**

- She will have money so she can start learning how to invest. Investing is one of the major 'missing pieces' in many financial education programs. Children are taught about saving and balancing checkbooks (which practically no one does anymore because they just check their balances on the internet) but they are not always taught about investing in assets that will produce passive income (cash flow) for them.

- She'll learn that saving to purchase an item she really wants isn't as difficult as it may seem, at first, if she uses a system. She will feel great when she reaches her savings goals and gets to purchase the item she's budgeted for.

- She will have money for continued education, regardless of her age.

- She is less likely to develop the habit of feeling guilty about spending her own money.

- She will understand the joy and importance of giving back and helping others so that when she has a lot more money than she needs each month, she will hopefully want to do great things with it because she has experienced this excitement from a young age.

Isn't it worth the extra money to help her learn these valuable lessons? We hope you think so. Parents who use this system say it actually SAVES them money in the long run. Think about it...if your son or daughter runs out of money and asks you for more, you simply say, "You have your own money. Can I help you manage it better next week (or month)?"

NOTES:

THE FINAL AGREEMENTS

"Real integrity is doing the right thing, knowing that nobody's going to know whether you did it or not." ~ OPRAH WINFREY

Three of the most important values that we can instill in a child are honesty, integrity and authenticity and one of the main ways these three values show up is how we keep agreements with ourselves and others. As we get older, we are constantly making agreements with others; from simple ones like calling a friend at 9:00 p.m. on Friday, to more complicated agreements such as finishing projects by a certain date or time. It used to be that when someone gave someone else their 'word' on something, it was their bond, literally. Then along came the attorneys...

The United States is the most litigious country in the world and Americans sue others for 'doing things to them' more frequently than any other country. Why this is so requires a discussion much deeper than I am prepared to go into in this book. The next step, however, does lend itself to providing your child with an opportunity to learn about contracts, making an agreement, and learning that one can usually re-negotiate an agreement as well.

On pages 102 and 103, you'll see two *Ultimate Allowance Contracts* that you will present to your child. Signing these contracts may be the first time your child signs his name on a dotted line. Help him realize that he is now signing a legal document that holds him accountable to what is written on the agreement.

Simply read through the agreements (contracts) with your child, fill in the blanks and sign them if you are both in agreement. Let the child know that though they are binding contracts, making a new agreement or modifying the agreement is always possible, if both parties agree. Point out that it is always best to make a new agreement *before* you break the old agreement.

Once the agreements are signed, use the blank worksheets on pages 104 and 105 to figure your child's allowance.

ULTIMATE ALLOWANCE CONTRACTS

Child's Agreement with Parent

I _____ (child) agree that it is MY responsibility to use my Ultimate Allowance in the best ways possible with the information I have at the time.

I agree to ask for guidance when I need it.

I agree to use my Money Jars at all times.

I know the Ultimate Allowance will help me grow up and handle my money wisely. It is my goal to grow up Financially Free!

Child's Signature: _____

Date: _____

ULTIMATE ALLOWANCE CONTRACTS

Parent's Agreement with Child

I _____ (parent) agree to
provide _____(child)
with an Ultimate Allowance amount of $_____
on a _____ (weekly, bi-weekly, monthly) basis
distributed on _____ (day or date) to
be used wisely to provide for those things agreed upon in
Worksheet A, including use of the Money Jar System. I
promise to be supportive and teach you how to manage
and use your money wisely.

The next scheduled evaluation of the program is (insert
date) _____.

Parent/Guardian Signature: _____

Parent/Guardian Signature: _____

Date: _____

For additional contracts, please download them at:

www.ultimateallowancebook.com/UAB/UAContracts.pdf

Worksheet A

Use this worksheet to figure out what you are spending on your child each month. Do this activity with your child.

CHILD'S NAME: _____ AGE: _____ DATE: _____

Item or Activity	Cost per month in Jar						Want/Need
	L	F	S	E	P	D	
							W N
							W N
							W N
							W N
							W N
							W N
							W N
							W N
							W N
							W N
							W N
							W N
							W N
							W N
							W N
							W N
							W N
							W N
							W N
							W N
							W N
JAR TOTALS							=

L=Living, F=FREEDOM, S=Saving, E=Education, P=Play, D=Donation

Worksheet B

MONEY JAR	TOTAL PER JAR	ADULT JAR %
Living Jar		55%
FREEDOM Jar		10%
Saving Jar		10%
Education Jar		10%
Play Jar		10%
Donation Jar		5%
JAR & % TOTALS	$ _____	_____ %

Next, add up each jar column (L, F, S, E, P, D) on Worksheet A and put the totals of each jar into the middle column on Worksheet B.

Put the total $ of all the jars in the last row of the middle column.

Circle the jars that are used in the right hand column.

Add up the percentages that are circled and put them into the bottom row of the right hand column.

Now, figure out your child's total Ultimate Allowance as follows:

Jar Total ($) divided by Jar % Total = Ultimate Allowance

$_____ / _____ % = _____
Jar Total   Jar % Total   Ultimate Allowance Total

Lastly, using the Ultimate Allowance Total, figure the amount you're going to give based on how often you've decided to provide it:

_____WEEKLY   = TOTAL DIVIDED BY 4

_____BI-WEEKLY   = TOTAL DIVIDED BY 2

_____MONTHLY   = TOTAL AMOUNT

For a downloadable version of this worksheet, please visit:

www.ultimateallowancebook.com/UAB/UltimateSheet.pdf

MAKING IT WORK

*"If you must play, decide on three things at the start:
the rules of the game, the stakes, and the quitting time."*
~ CHINESE PROVERB

Knowing something and doing something are two totally different things. Doing requires, in a sense, *being* a certain way and, in order to implement and maintain the Ultimate Allowance system, you're going to have to *be* the kind of parent or guardian who knows what is best for your child and *be able* to hold steady the course, regardless of what's happening along the way.

You must be able to see the bigger picture; visualize the results that you want to create in the future and *be willing to do what is necessary to make that happen*. After all this effort, and assuming all goes as planned, you will *have* an adult child who is financially responsible.

I'm going to assume that since you've made it this far through this book, you have the desire to *be* the person who can empower your kids with financial habits and tools that will prepare them to lead happy, fulfilled lives. This next section will help make sure you have the tools and information you need to make the *commitment* necessary to make it happen. No one said parenting was easy. And it is my belief that loving them isn't enough. Preparing our children to be wise, responsible adults takes our love, time, energy and commitment to them. Preparing them to handle money wisely takes nothing less.

The most important part of all, having *faith* in both your ability to create success with this program and your child's ability to learn and

BE • DO • HAVE

We teach a concept in all of our programs called **Be, Do, Have.** For more information, please visit:

www.ultimateallowancebook.com/UAB/bedohave.pdf

embrace the information and habits, will come in time. Right now, though you think and feel that this system makes great sense to you, you may still be questioning whether it will work for your family. That's normal when starting any new program or system of growth or education.

Where you're going to really need to have faith is in the middle. If your child is one of the rare ones who constantly complains (usually because they don't want to be responsible) or it just seems like a lot of work to maintain the system, we invite you to come back to this next section and revisit WHY you decided to implement this system in the first place. Hopefully re-reading your words will give you the encouragement you need to get back on the road, helping your child create his own financial freedom in the future.

THE MOST IMPORTANT PIECE OF THIS PUZZLE

You, the parents or guardian, are the most important ingredient in this program for it to be a success. A plan is only a plan; a system is only a system unless you commit to DOING it, not just TRYING it. Yoda from Star Wars said, *"There is do, or do not...there is no try."*

As I've said, some children embrace this program right off the bat, while others simply don't want to be responsible or despise the idea of spending their own money so badly that they constantly complain. Regardless of the response your child has, there are a few critical steps you can take that will help ensure everyone's success. The first step in any process should be setting goals and intentions. If you're ready, let's move on to the goals.

STEP 1...Setting Goals

"A goal is just a dream with a deadline."
~ UNKNOWN

Setting goals and intentions for this program, for both you and your child, will help everyone stay focused on these goals. One of the most important aspects of accomplishing goals is the process of *writing them down on a regular basis*. Studies have shown that people who write down their goals on a regular basis accomplish their goals; people who don't, usually don't.

Another important aspect of reaching goals is being able to see, and feel, the goal already accomplished. Think in terms of both short-term and long-term goals. The following questions will help you understand and formulate your goals for the program. The first few questions are for you, the next set is for your child.

1. In general, what would you like to see in your child as a result of this program, in terms of:

BEHAVIORS?_____

_____

_____

_____

_____

HABITS?_____

_____

_____

_____

_____

OTHER RESULTS?_____

_____

_____

_____

_____

_____

2. Are you committed to doing this program, knowing that it is going to take your...

TIME?	____YES ____NO
ENERGY?	____YES ____NO
COMMITMENT?	____YES ____NO
DEDICATION?	____YES ____NO

3. Are both parents (or guardians) onboard and committed to this system?   ____Yes ____No

4. If the answer to question #3 is No, does the non-supportive parent agree to let the supportive parent be in charge of implementing the program?   ____Yes ____No

5. What kinds of things can you think of that may keep you and your child from succeeding with this program?

_____

_____

_____

_____

_____

_____

6. If any of the above happened, what can you do to regain control and get more support?

_____

_____

_____

_____

7. Who else in your extended network of family and friends might be able to lend support?

_____

_____

_____

GOOD JOB!

The previous questions will help ensure everyone's success, and keep you on task, as you implement this system. To further enroll your child in this process, it's important that he also be encouraged to set his own goals and intentions. Remember, it's important that this system is his, not yours.

Next, sit down with your child and have him answer this next set of questions. I do recommend that if you are implementing this system with more than one child at a time, do this section with each.

1. Why do you think it might be important for you to learn how to use money wisely?

_____

_____

_____

_____

2. What kind of life do you think you would have if you didn't learn about money?

_____

_____

_____

3. What would you like to learn about money?

_____

_____

_____

_____

4. Do you talk to your friends about money? ____Yes ____No

5. If Yes, what do you talk about?

_____

_____

_____

6. Complete the following sentence with one of these options.

I'D LIKE TO GROW UP AND...(CIRCLE ONE)

Option A	Option B	Option C
...not have enough money to live on every month.	...have just enough money to live on every month.	...have plenty of money to live the lifestyle I choose.

One of the most important concepts you and your children can learn is that financial freedom is a *choice*. When asked, most adults say they never *chose* to be rich or middle class or poor. They just assumed life happened to them. The fact is that *not* making a choice is making a choice to let life just happen with no forethought or planning; no design and little direction. Teaching your kids the importance of choosing what they want early on will make a tremendous difference for them later on.

> ## CREATIVE WEALTH PRINCIPLE
> Financial Freedom is Your Choice!

Use the following metaphors to explain to your kids that there are two primary ways they can approach life: as a firefighter or as an architect. Once they understand the difference, most kids realize that life doesn't happen the way they want it to unless they start making choices. Choosing financial freedom is a great place to start!

LIFE AS A FIRE FIGHTER

A firefighter lets life affect him; in other words, he thinks life just happens *to* him. He's always reacting to life, putting out fires, rescuing himself and others from situations, always at the effect of life. Most firefighters are constantly tired and stressed from putting out all the fires, solving all the problems that seem to come their way. They don't learn that their lives are just a result of all their choices. Their lives seems to be full of drama, with things going 'wrong' all the time. They rarely stop to ask why.

NOTE: Firefighters are GREAT! Where would we be without them? Firefighters save lives and rescue people, pets and things for us, so please don't get the idea that fire fighting, as a career, is an issue.

LIFE AS AN ARCHITECT

An architect, on the other hand, spends time designing the life he wants, right down to every detail. He knows what he wants to do in life, knows what he enjoys, knows that his thoughts, beliefs and attitudes dictate how his life unfolds. He visualizes the life he wants and knows exactly how it's going to feel.

Empowering a child or teen to make the choices necessary to create a particular lifestyle takes patience, forethought and constant unconditional love and acceptance. When our children come up to us and say they want to grow up and be a this or do that, as parents, we may instantly think to ourselves, "That's never going to happen." Perhaps what our children are really saying to us is, "Mom, Dad, I just want to know I can do anything I set my mind to."

I believe it's really important to encourage a child's enthusiasm, ideas, goals and dreams. Many children, just like many adults I know, are just dreaming out loud. I say, let them dream! We never know, and it's not our place to tell anyone that their dream won't work or come true.

Many parents feel that the toughest part of being a parent is saying NO. But what if rather than telling your child NO, you simply said, "Yes, when..." or, "Yes, if..." or even, "Yes, as soon as..."? The Ultimate Allowance system allows you to use this technique so your child always feels empowered. If your son or daughter wants something or wants to do something (aside from buying a gun or jumping off a bridge, of course), you can simply say, "Sure, when you've got enough money in your Play Jar," or, "Absolutely, as soon as your Education Jar has that much money in it."

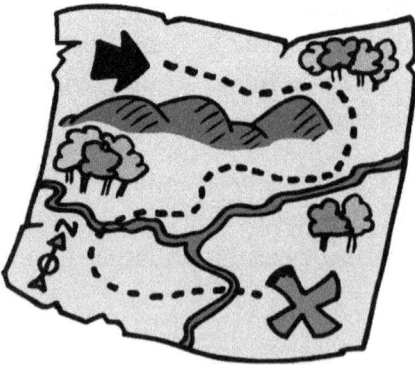

What makes this program so effective is that your child will continually have hands-on learning experiences that you couldn't begin to think up if you tried.

Your job, as the parent or guardian, is to be there to guide, congratulate, console, listen and fully support him as he meanders through this new and unchartered territory called **Financial Self-Reliance**.

You see, on this journey to Financial Self-Reliance, your child may choose to travel through any one, or more, of the following places...

Buyer's Remorse Avenue • Deprivation Drive • Saver's Street • Begging Boulevard • Tempted Alley • Convincing Court • Overspending Overlook • Keeping Up With Lane • Accumulation Corner • Rebellion Circle • Responsibility Highway • The Ocean of Emotion • R.O.I. River • Debt Valley • Motivation Mountain • Temptation Trail • Piddlyjunk Place • Quicksand Creek • Liability Lake • Asset Airport • Passive Income Freeway and finally arrive at his own **Financial Freedom Frontier**. You may even recognize a few of these places yourself!

You must be available to help your child navigate this journey, just as you were there when she took her first steps and learned to walk.

This journey is a lot like when you first learned to drive a car; your children are going to hit a few bumps, make some terrible turns, and if they are like me, tear a little side molding off the truck on a fence post. But I lived through it and my Dad didn't get too mad because after all, it was just the farm truck. Slowly but surely, however, I learned to miss the posts, look both ways, evaluate and navigate the curves and eventually drive my Mom to the store (even though secretly she was still probably scared to death).

In reality, it *is* just a small amount of money the kids are 'playing' with relative to the amounts they will be responsible for as adults. Just remember that you're preparing them for successful adulthood and, bottom line, that always takes money.

CREATIVE WEALTH PRINCIPLE
People Aren't Judged By Their Abilities but By the Sum of Their Choices.

NOTES:

STEP 2...PROPER PRIOR PLANNING

"Good plans shape good decisions. That's why good planning helps to make elusive dreams come true."

~ LESTER R. BITTEL, *The Nine Master Keys of Management*

I've heard it said that **LUCK** is what happens when **PREPARATION** meets **OPPORTUNITY**.

Well, I think you may want to plan for a little luck along the way. Don't worry, I'm going to help you by preparing you to handle whatever comes up, and especially, by preparing you for what to say to your child in a variety of different circumstances.

We've provided some examples for many scenarios, just in case. Sometimes we (adults) say the worst possible thing at the worst possible moment simply because we aren't prepared and we haven't thought through exactly what would bring about the best response or result in certain situations.

How many of us have said something to someone only to walk away and think of the perfect response just minutes later? Or worse, felt badly because we said something that offended or made the person feel terrible about himself or something he did?

I've also learned that as our emotion goes up, our ability to act and think intelligently goes down proportionately.

I couldn't agree more, and on that note, we want YOU to be prepared to handle the following situations like a pro.

1) **What to say when you introduce the Ultimate Allowance System to your child.**

2) **What to say if your child rebels and says it's too hard or he doesn't want to be responsible anymore.**

3) **What to say and do when your child spends more money than he's supposed to on that new pair of hot running shoes all the guys are wearing and then doesn't have enough money to pay for the socks to go with those shoes.**

4) What to say when your child won't stop begging for something he wants because he thinks YOU should pay for it.

5) What to say when your child has great success saving, investing, starting a business, improving his education, donating to her favorite charity (and how to pick one), enjoying his play money, etc.

NOTES:

Step 3...Introducing the Program

"For every person who wants to teach there are approximately thirty people who don't want to learn—much."
~ W. C. SELLAR AND R. J. YEATMAN

As adults and parents, most of us realize that, in life, there are teachable moments when we are open and receptive to relevant information, and there are moments when it doesn't matter who is attempting to teach us, we are simply not willing, or able, to take in the information.

Children are no different. You probably know that sometimes it's just flat out impossible to get your kids to learn something (or even listen) as long as *you* are the one who is doing the teaching. But have a friend introduce an idea or concept to them and they are open and receptive to the information.

With the Ultimate Allowance, you will be the one introducing the program, walking your child through it and helping her every step of the way as she learns how to master this *money game thing* through trial and error. Therefore, it is critical that you introduce it correctly, and at the best possible moment.

First, find a time when it makes sense to bring it up. Right after they've had a fight with a friend or lost a valuable toy or broken a vase is not that time! I've heard it said that people don't change until the pain of change is less than the pain of staying the same. Watch for a time when your child has had, or is about to have, an experience involving money. It can be either a positive or negative experience; you never can tell when a child will be receptive to new information.

When you're deciding on the perfect time to introduce this system, here are two questions you might ask yourself first:

119

1. **Is what I want to talk about with my child relevant to the current situation?**

2. **Will the information I'm about to present provide a solution to a problem or situation my child is experiencing?**

If the answer to these questions is Yes, then you probably have a teachable moment on your hands.

THE DIFFERENCES BETWEEN BOYS AND GIRLS

Money means different things to boys than it does to girls; and later, to men and women. The most important thing to remember is that girls and boys often think differently about money and as with most things in life, this is what I call a 'genderalization' so if it doesn't fit you or your child, that's OK.

What I have noticed in my adult programs is that men and women are often driven often completely different financial value systems. Girls think about money in terms of security and independence. Boys think about it in terms of power, prestige and the ability to provide for others.

Another distinction is that girls usually collect things and boys usually trade things. This trait shows up in how they deal with money both as kids and as adults. Girls will use money to collect clothes and shoes; boys will use money to trade cards, toys and then property.

Finally, remember that even today, our society appears to value the creative ideas of boys and men more than those of girls and women. Quite often, if a boy comes up with an idea to make money, he is praised and encouraged to proceed with that idea, but if a girl comes up with a similar idea, people tend to say how cute they think she is or the idea is. This is very interesting in light of the current trend which says that more small businesses are being started by women in the United States.

Just be careful and watch how you speak to your children when dealing with money. You may notice that you are actually treating them differently.

WHAT TO SAY AND HOW TO SAY IT

"Constantly talking isn't necessarily communicating."
~ CHARLIE KAUFMAN

Now that you understand the system, it's time to actually spill the beans to your kids. The accelerated teaching techniques I've mentioned before provide all sorts of communications skills that are great for parenting and one of them is *Ask Don't Tell*. So often we just want to teach using the *Sit and Listen to Me Lecture to You* method. My experience over the past several years, however, tells me that kids of all ages (adults included) know the answers, or at least have a good feel for them. Before you start talking *at* them, *ask* them about the subject matter instead.

It's important to make what you're about to say *relevant* to your kids in some way. If it isn't, they won't listen. I've found it best to use another one of the powerful techniques we use in all of our programs called *Enrolling Questions*. Enrolling Questions help us engage and enroll people of all ages in the learning process.

As the name implies, this technique involves figuring out how to *enroll* the child in what you're about to teach him, i.e. get him excited, engaged, listening and wanting more. It's critical when you're working with a *group* of kids to enroll 100% of them. Sometimes you have to ask several enrolling questions to get 100% but, in the end, it's worth the effort.

Enrolling questions look something like this:

Q. How would you like to learn a way to make sure you always have money for things like that (meaning something they want you to purchase for them)?

Q. How would you like to make sure you always have plenty of money for the things you want and need?

Q. How powerful would it feel to be in charge of your own money instead of me controlling it?

Q. Picture this...what if I told you that I have an idea that will make it so you never have to ask me for money again?

Q. How would you like to learn how to take care of your own money now so this never happens again?

Q. How would you like to grow up and work because you want to, not because you have to?

Q. I see you like to help people. What if I could show you a way to have enough money to help anyone you wanted?

Q. How would it feel if...(fill in the blank with any kind of situation or scenario you'd like to paint for the child that you know she might want or enjoy).

Q. What would happen if...

Q. How would you like to...

Q. Imagine what would happen if...

Q. Imagine what it would be like if you could always...

You get the idea. An enrolling question gives just enough information to make the other party interested in what you're about to say, but doesn't give away the punch line (the subject matter). Remember, sometimes you have to ask several enrolling questions to get a person's interest at any given time. (Psst. This technique works great in our adult relationships as well!)

Since you know your child's interests, passions and hot buttons better than anyone else, it should be fairly easy to come up with a few enrolling questions that will get his attention and get him to ask, "How could I do that?" or "What do you mean?" or "Can you tell me more?" Any probing question on his part means he wants more information and you've hooked him.

NOTE: If you're introducing the system to several of your children at the same time, you'll want to figure out a few questions that will enroll them all. Once you have them hooked, sit them down and introduce the system in a way that will answer the questions that you just asked to enroll them.

NOTE: Give yourself a Brownie Point here because sometimes hooking them is the trickiest part!

EXPLAINING THE PROGRAM

"We have, as human beings, a storytelling problem. We're a bit too quick to come up with explanations for things we don't really have an explanation for."
~ MALCOLM GLADWELL, author of
Blink: The Power of Thinking Without Thinking

Now that you have them hooked, what exactly can you say to your kids to explain to them that their lives are about to change dramatically, and you're doing it for their own good? In other words, how do you explain to them that they are about to take on a lot more responsibility than they may want at this point in their lives, and make it sound like a great idea? That's easy...you just say, "Because I'm the parent and I said so!"

OK, that's what my Dad always said and it didn't work with me, either. Let's look at some more encouraging approaches.

> *"Susie, your Dad and I want you to be able to take care of yourself when you grow up and one of the things we all have to know is how to use money wisely. We just read this incredible book and think it's great. We think you'll like it, too. It's called the Ultimate Allowance and it works like this..."*

or

> *"Well, you know how you always have to ask me (or your...) for money every time you want something or want to go somewhere and do something with your friends? I/We found a way so you never have to do that again. It's called the Ultimate Allowance and this is how it works..."*

or

> *"You know, no one ever taught me (us) about money when I was your age and I've had to learn the hard way. (You might want to add your own story here to make it more personal). Well, I don't want that to happen to you because I just don't think it's fair that you leave home not knowing how to use money wisely. So, I*

125

looked around and discovered this fun system called the Ultimate Allowance and I want to share it with you. It's something we do together and it works like this."

Remember to do your best to tie your explanation to the enrolling questions you used to get them interested (hooked) in the first place.

Let's continue to explain the program to your child.

"The Ultimate Allowance works like this. You know that I (we) spend money to support you; things you need like clothes, shoes, lessons, school supplies, food and things like that, right? Great. And you know how you're always coming to me (us) for money to buy things you want or to go to a movie with a friend or to buy ice cream or something, right? Great. And you know how when you want something you also do your best to get me (us) to buy it for you? Well, what would you say if you didn't ever have to ask me for money again? How would it feel to be in charge of paying for all your own things? The Ultimate Allowance makes it so you can do just that, and it's fun and easy.

"What we're going to do is learn it together, use a few worksheets and walk through the system so that from now on YOU are in charge of some (or all, depending on what age your child is when you introduce the system to her) of your expenses (explain what an expense is if you need to).

"But that's not all. Remember when we talked about how it might be important some day for you to understand how money works and how you can grow up and have more than enough to live the way you want to? Well, the Ultimate Allowance includes something called Money Jars that show you what to do with all your money now so you'll know what to do with it when you grow up. How does that sound? Great, let's figure it out together. I sure wish someone had taught me this information when I was your age!"

Now, just a reminder that you may have one of those kids who gets fearful at the thought of having to be responsible for his own money, let alone a lot of yours. You'll need to start this child off very slowly, making him or her responsible for just a few little expenses and purchases in the beginning. Hopefully, over time, with the help of the jars, and the rest of the program, he will develop some financial self-esteem and feel empowered by his new responsibilities, skills and habits.

By now, you should have your child's interest and buy-in to the system. Once this happens, simply follow the steps outlined on page 96.

THE WHY: COMPOUNDING INTEREST & GROWTH

"The most powerful force in the Universe is compound interest."
"Compounding is the 8th wonder of the world."
~ ALBERT EINSTEIN

Part of explaining this system to your kids and getting their buy-in, remember, is showing them the *why*. You have to get them to see the value of starting early and why when they do start early, it's easy. In other words, we have to show them the *time value of money*. As I've mentioned before, one of the most powerful things you can show a child is the power of compound interest and compound growth.

Compound interest is money you make when someone else uses your money, like when you put money into a savings account, CD (certificate of deposit), money market account or loan money to someone for some purpose and charge them interest. Your money is making money for you...kinda like *it* getting the second job.

Compound growth is often what causes your investments to increase in value, and it's not always *interest* that causes this growth.

For example, with a mutual fund where you are reinvesting your dividends (part of the company's profits), those dividends buy you more shares in the mutual fund. This is compound growth but it isn't interest per se that is causing the growth. The growth is caused by the increase in the value of the underlying stock that the mutual fund is invested in.

Do the activity on the next page with your child to show them the most important *why* in investing. The answers are on page 209 of this book.

THE MAGIC OF COMPOUND INTEREST

If you spend $10 per week on things you think you don't need (piddlyjunk), can you imagine what that $10 would be worth if you started investing it instead?

$10 x 52 weeks per year = $520 per year

If you invested that $10 a week instead of spending it, for 50 years (from age 15-65), at the average interest or rate of return for the stock market (10%), guess how much money you would have at age 65? What would you have with a 12% return on your investment?

$167,083 $1,200,000

$756,979

$26,000

$1,709,453

Write your answer here (10%): _____

Write your answer here (12%): _____

It's Magic!

WHAT TO DO WHEN...

...THEY MAKE A GREAT CHOICE

This is the best time of all! Sarah Singer-Nourie, in the book she coauthored on accelerated learning called *Quantum Teaching*, likes to say, "If it's worth learning, it's worth celebrating."

A pat on the back and a rousing, "Great job!" is the first place to start when it comes to making children feel great about themselves and their choices. They learn to associate great money choices with positive reactions from you and others, but best of all, they associate these great choices with positive feelings within themselves.

In addition to celebrating a really big win with them when they make a great choice, you might reward your child with the following:

- A special night out for dinner, a movie, ice cream, concert, or some other activity they enjoy.

- A bonus to put into their FREEDOM Jar: cash, shares of stock in their name, etc.

- Something they love, like a new book, art supplies, etc.

A couple of points: I'd refrain from celebrating with the purchase of piddlyjunk because the message there is, "Spend money when you feel good," and that's not the message you want them to take into adulthood. I'd also suggest that they invite a friend to help them celebrate, thereby setting a great example for the friend also.

Again, save the special celebrating for times when they've had a really great success or win, not every time, or they'll learn to save and invest because they are being externally rewarded. We want them to be motivated internally for life so they'll manage their money wisely just because.

...THEY MAKE A POOR CHOICE (I.E., A MISTAKE)

I truly believe that, for the most part, kids don't get up in the morning and ask themselves, "I wonder how I can mess up my life (or my parent's life) today?" Mistakes are just their way (and our way) of learning about the world. Kids generally want to do their best, just like us. Remember, we are generally all doing our best with the information we have at the time.

When kids do make mistakes, we have a choice in how we respond. Some responses tend to make kids defensive—causing them to hold back or lie to you—while other responses help create kids who easily and happily learn from their mistakes.

Kids who fear punishment, or the loss of love, in response to their mistakes, learn to hide their mistakes. These children live in two different places: one where they have the love and support of their parents, and another where they feel that if their mistakes were discovered, they would be undeserving of that love. It's hard for these kids to fully accept their parents' love and support even when it is expressed. It's also difficult for these kids to set high standards for themselves, because they tend to be afraid of failing.

In life, there really are no failures, only learning opportunities, so please be careful with your words. One of my favorite sayings is that the only real failure in life is the failure to participate. I love this philosophy. What if kids were encouraged to try all sorts of different things and make mistakes in order to learn? What if we intentionally set them up for success every day? What a difference that would make in our society!

From my experience working with adults, many of them are so afraid of failing that they often won't even *try* new things; they don't feel good enough or worthy of success because of the way they were treated as kids.

Here are some suggestions if you are committed to raising kids who can learn from their mistakes, and you're not afraid of making a few of your own:

- Accept the idea that your kids are doing their best, and embrace the idea that they'll learn faster from their mistakes if they are in an environment that accepts mistakes. This means that you must set the example by not getting upset when you, yourself, make a poor choice. Let your children hear you say out loud, "Wow, that decision/choice didn't lead me in the direction I wanted to go. I wonder what I can learn from this?"

- If you're having difficulty (frustration or impatience) with your child's mistakes, understand that this may be a reflection of your difficulty in dealing with your own mistakes. Be aware of this connection and deal with your own issues first. Your frustration may also have to do with your 'expectations' of your child's behavior. I heard a wonderful saying once, "Expectations are resentments under construction." I think that says it all.

  Remember that our children aren't in this world to do as WE please. They are here to grow up and be their own unique person.

- Learn to recognize the negative shaming messages that we can easily give to our kids without realizing it. These messages can do a lot of damage and make them feel unworthy. Here's a few of them:

      "You should be ashamed of yourself."

      "How could you have done that?"

      "You don't listen to me!"

      "That was a dumb question."

      "What were you thinking?"

      "How you could be so stupid?"

      "You can do better than that!"

"What's the matter with you?"

"Why can't you be like your sister or brother?"

- Continually provide your kids with learning experiences, and at the same time, structure their environment so they can't make too many mistakes. For example, consider providing their allowance once a week if they have been getting it once a month, rather than giving them a whole months' worth of money to deal with at once if they seem to be struggling.

- Again, provide a great role model for your children by the way you react when you make your own mistakes. Do you get defensive and stretch the truth, or do you "own" the mistake and learn something from it? Create an environment at home that's based on learning from mistakes.

There are plenty of daily opportunities to show our kids the patience, acceptance and discipline it takes to allow us all to learn from our mistakes. Give your kids the room they need and deserve so that they can learn organically; in other words, let them learn by doing and experiencing. Sometimes, it's not just the choices you make, but what you make of the choices.

Some things you can say to your child are:

"It's perfectly OK to make a poor choice. It's how I have learned some of my biggest lessons in life. I remember one time when I _____ (fill in the blank . . . give him a personal example to relate to)."

Then ask, "So, what did you learn from this choice?"

Don't make what they chose or did wrong (notice the word 'poor' in the sentence above) and don't give them more lesson than they are ready for. One good lesson learned per mistake is about all kids can handle. (It's about all adults can handle, too.)

Another option:

"Hey, I make mistakes myself. Everyone I know makes mistakes. Big deal. Fact is, no one who is great ever got great without making a lot of mistakes. It's how we learn."

"Would you like to talk about some other options you might be able to choose next time?"

And yet another:

"I know how you feel. I remember when I used to do _____ when I was your age. Boy, what a bummer. I can totally relate."

Really get on their level and help them feel like you really *do* relate to their experience (and mean it). Let them know it's OK, no one is perfect, and tell them there's a reason the front windshield in a car is bigger than the rear view mirror: we need to spend most of our time looking forward, not backward. A couple of fun sayings to instill are:

"Live and learn."

and

"Correct and continue."

A note about the power of words: It is my personal belief that words are powerful. I also believe they can mean nothing and everything, all at the same time; it just depends on what you make them mean. Because we *do* tend to make them mean more than they usually mean, do your best to refrain from using the word 'mistake.' Frame your children's actions and behaviors as a choice that didn't lead toward a desired goal or use the terms supportive and nonsupportive.

Some of this information was found at:

www.markbrandenburg.com

...WHEN THEY ASK YOU TO PAY FOR SOMETHING

This situation is bound to happen. Remember *Conclusion Number Two*: children would rather spend *your* money than theirs. If they think there's a good chance that you'll buy something for them that they haven't saved for, they are liable to ask you to do it over and over and over again.

133

While there's nothing wrong with occasionally buying something extra for your child, just remember your intention for this program: preparing your child for financial self-reliance. If you continually buy things for your children, they are not learning how to be self-reliant.

When you DO decide to buy something for your child:

1) Don't do it when they are begging; and,

2) Work out a cooperative plan with your child. For instance, you could agree to pay for a portion of the purchase and they save up for the rest, or they agree on some other type of exchange for helping them purchase something they want.

NEVER, I repeat NEVER agree to loan your child an advance on their allowance, unless, of course, you charge them interest!

Let there be lessons in it all. If you loan them money without charging them interest, you are teaching them how to use credit cards without the card. If you want to go one step further, have them sign a promissory note, as well. My Mom always did this with me and you can imagine how official it always felt. There was NO way I would have ever missed a payment or not paid her back. And, I might add, that she never hesitated loaning me money!

I also think it's fine to buy kids something special if you're away on a trip or you just see something that you know they would love. We all love surprises.

...THEY REBEL OR COMPLAIN

As I've said, occasionally there is a child, typically a Money Monk or an Avoider in the making, who just doesn't want to deal with the whole issue of money. It's usually a matter of not wanting the responsibility that comes along with it or their being so busy or focused elsewhere that they don't want to deal with it. If this is the case with your child, there are some things you can do.

First, do what you can to uncover the root of the problem. Even children have the beginnings of deep-seated beliefs about money, and although most children crave independence, many of them are scared to death of the idea of taking care of themselves. (This is also one of the reasons adult children move back in with their parents, or never leave in the first place.)

A couple of questions to consider:

1) Is your child responsible for too many things in his life already?

2) Is he involved in too many activities and can't deal with the idea of one more thing to handle?

3) Has she watched you or someone else express negative emotions or anger in regard to the responsibilities around money and financial matters?

The answers to these questions may give you some insights into your child's unwillingness or inability to embrace the idea of taking care of his own money needs.

When approaching a child who just flat out doesn't want to deal with money, some well thought out questions leading to a nonemotional conversation (on your side) might just tip the scales in your favor. Ask him what money means to him. Ask him what his life would be without money. Ask him who is going to handle the money when he gets older, and other questions like these. If you still don't get anywhere with your child, elicit the help of one of your child's adult friends; an uncle, aunt, friend or teacher. You never know who may have access to the inner workings of your child's mind and heart.

Again, do your best to uncover the *why*. Then you'll know how to help him through the challenge and gently ease him into a life of financial responsibility. Keep in mind this isn't a life or death issue (at this point) so take your time and gradually you'll find the answers. The most important thing to remember is to create a safe place where the child can talk and express his thoughts and feelings about money and taking care of his own financial needs.

...WHEN THEY RUN OUT OF MONEY

It's bound to happen; children make poor choices just like we do. A great way to handle this situation is to ask questions:

1) How do you feel about choosing to spend your money that way?

2) How does it feel to not have enough money left over to pay for the things you need to pay for?

3) What are the consequences of this choice?

4) Didn't you make an agreement to budget your money so you could pay for the things we agreed you'd pay for?

5) What do you think I should do to help you?

6) Is there something that influenced the decision that led to this situation?

7) How can I support you in the future so this doesn't happen again?

8) What did you learn from this choice?

9) Would you like to make a new agreement?

10) So, what are you going to do now?

And so forth. Unless it's an emergency, my advice is: don't bail him out. You must let him experience the consequences of making a poor financial choice or the lesson will be lost. One of the belief systems you don't want to foster is that someone is always going to be there to rescue him. This is a common belief that parents instill in their children by the responses they make when their children make poor financial choices. It does not serve your children to rescue them. Our number one principle in all of our programs is:

Please don't chastise or criticize him either. He knows he made a poor choice (the words *poor choice* hold less judgment than *bad choice*). As I keep saying, we all make mistakes, and we stress in our all of our camps and programs that financial freedom is your responsibility and it's all simply a matter of making choices. These times are the perfect times for your kids to start really paying attention to all of the financial choices they make, big and small.

If you're lucky, the idea of life being the sum of their choices will transfer to other areas of their lives; relationships, attitudes, school, fitness, health and more. This is how we create responsible adults instead of victims.

Now that we've introduced the program, found great ways to enroll them into the system and dealt with the fallout, if any, the next step is teaching your kids how to make wise, supportive choices that lead *toward* their goals instead of *away* from them.

SAVING & SPENDING PLAN OR SSP

As you might imagine, one of the backbones of any financial literacy program is learning the power of knowing where your money goes. A good majority of adults, if asked, can't tell you where they spent the last $100 they had in cash. And I know this because I ask them. It's just so easy to spend cash or hand a store clerk your ATM card without logging the expenditure somewhere (a checkbook register comes to mind). We have another financial power tool in our programs that shows your kids how to plan where their money goes. It's called a *Saving and Spending Plan*, or SSP for short.

Most adults cringe at the mere mention of the word BUDGET; maybe because it feels like a financial DIET and we all know how well diets work. However, when we do this activity with our kids and teens in our camps, it's amazing how they all say they didn't know it was going to be so difficult to figure out where to put their money. (Funny, that's just what most of our adults say!) A budget is simply another tool to help you reach your dreams, and when it's put that way, even adults begin to see the value of creating and sticking with one!

Since your child has money allocated for his different Money Jars now, he will be deciding how best to spend, save and invest his allowance. We've included the SSP activity from our camp program here, because it has proven to be so valuable for both kids and parents.

Do the activity on the following pages 140-140 with your child. (Completed worksheet on page 207) See if he can make the money cover everything he needs and wants. If he's like the kids in our programs, he'll be very surprised at how hard it is. Most kids think that $3000 a month is a lot of money, until they do this activity, that is.

NOTE: Explain Fixed Expenses and Variable Expenses. Ask the child if she knows what the terms are before you tell her. Examples of fixed expenses are house payments, rent payments and car payments. Examples of variable expenses are food, utility bills and clothing.

CREATIVE WEALTH PRINCIPLE

It's Better to Tell Your Money Where To Go,
Than To Ask It Where It Went.

Make sure you do a new SSP each time you re-evaluate the program; this gives your child the opportunity to watch life get more expensive and gives both of you practice evaluating income and expenditures over time.

NOTE: If your son or daughter has trouble staying within their allowance, tell them they have two choices:

1) Spend less money then they make, or

2) Make more than they spend.

Then, simply ask him or her this question:

Q. If you don't want to spend less, what can you do to make more money?

You might be surprised at what comes out of their mouths!

CREATIVE WEALTH PRINCIPLE

Spend Less Money Than You Make!

INVESTING THEIR FREEDOM JAR MONEY

"Pay Yourself First."

~ EVERY FINANCIALLY FREE PERSON ON EARTH!

So now your kids have money in their Freedom Jar and they want to know what they can do with it. Here are some ideas.

We teach kids the concept of investing in the **Three Pillars of Wealth**: business, the stock market and real estate. These are the ASSETS that most wealthy people invest in to create financial freedom for themselves. In other words, investing in these types of assets helps them create, over time, streams of Residual or Passive Income or cash flow (income they eventually don't have to trade their time and energy for) so they have money coming in when, and if, they decide to stop working for a living. With enough passive income coming in, people can work because they want to, not because they have to. And as I've mentioned, with more money coming in than we need each month, we can do a whole lot of good with the extra.

There are plenty of kids and teens out there who have started businesses and turned them into fully functioning, profit-making enterprises when they got out of high school or college. This is one of the reasons it's so important to encourage their entrepreneurial ideas while they are young! With the advent of the internet, there's an unlimited number of ways people can make money. Hey, maybe you could end up helping them run their companies!

For more incredible ideas on how to create financial freedom sooner than later (for you and your kids), please read Timothy Ferris's, *The 4-Hour Work Week* and Pat O'Bryan's, *Your Portable Empire.*

These two books will expose you to more new ideas about creating multiple streams of income than you ever dreamed possible. Literally, the sky's the limit!

CREATIVE WEALTH PRINCIPLE
Make Money Work By Putting It To Work For You.

SAVING AND SPENDING PLAN (AKA A BUDGET)

Unless you know where you are, it's hard to know how to get where you want to go. A Savings and Spending Plan puts you in charge and gives you a tool with which to reach your dreams. Let's assume you are making $3000 a month at your first real job. Let's fill in the blanks below and get started!

Gross Income/per month
❏ From Job . . . . $_____

Taxes/per month
❏ Federal, State, Social Security, Medicare (32%) . . $ _____

Net Income (take home pay)/per month
❏ Gross income minus taxes . . . . $_____

Your Money Jars
❏ Living Jar (55%) . . . . $_____
❏ FREEDOM Jar (10%) . . . . $_____
❏ Saving-Contingency Jar (10%) . . . . $_____
❏ Education Jar (10%) . . . . $_____
❏ Play Jar (10%) . . . . $_____
❏ Donation Jar (5%) . . . . $_____

Expenses

Turn to the next page and fill in the amount you think you might spend on the expenses listed. When you have finished, add up the total and put it in the box below and subtract it from your Living expenses total. If you have money left over, good job! If you didn't have enough, you'll need to go back and look over your expenses to see where you might cut back.

Living Expenses (fill in from above): . . . . $_____
Subtract your total expenses (from next page): . . . . . . $_____
Remainder, if any (put into your FREEDOM Jar!): . . . . . $_____

Other expenses you might not think of:

- Bank fees
- Bottled water
- Washing your car
- Dentist
- New tires

- Driver's license renewals
- Smog checks
- Laundromats
- Cover charges
- Coffee drinks/smoothies

- Gum
- Office supplies
- Emergencies
- Uniforms
- and on & on!!!

IT'S NOT AS EASY AS YOU MIGHT THINK!

TRY YOUR BUDGETING SKILLS - A REALITY CHECK

EXPENSES	Options ($)		AMOUNT ($)	Need or Want?	Fixed or Variable?
Shelter (Pick one)	Low	High	Your pick		
Apartment - 1 bedroom	$600	$1300		N W	F V
Apartment - share 2 bedroom	$400	$800		N W	F V
Rent room in home	$300	$1000		N W	F V
Transportation					
Car (used), w/insurance, gas	$250	$500		N W	F V
Bike	$10	$15		N W	F V
Public Transportation (bus, train)	$25	$100		N W	F V
Food					
Groceries (eat at home)	$250	$400		N W	F V
Eating out (in addition to groceries)	$25	$200		N W	
Utilities					F V
Phone	$30	$70		N W	F V
Cell phone	$50	$100		N W	F V
Electricity/Gas	$25	$200		N W	F V
Cable TV	$30	$100		N W	F V
Internet	$30	$40		N W	F V
Garbage/water (included in rent)	$0	$0	$0	N W	F V
Insurance					
Renter's	$10	$20		N W	F V
Health (usually provided by employer)	$150	$300	$0	N W	F V
Personal/Lifestyle					
Clothing	$50	$200		N W	F V
Entertainment (movies, concerts, games)	$20	$100		N W	F V
Hair cuts, manicures, etc.	$20	$60		N W	F V
Newspapers, books, magazines	$10	$25		N W	F V
Pets (food, vet, grooming)	$0	$25		N W	F V
Personal Hygiene (soap, shampoo)	$10	$30		N W	F V
Lessons (sports, music, dance, etc.)	$0	$300		N W	F V
Cleaning, household supplies	$20	$35		N W	F V
Vacation (yearly total/12 months)	$50	$200		N W	F V
Other				N W	F V
TOTAL					

Downloadable a copy of the SSP here:
www.ultimateallowancebook.com/UAB/ssp.pdf

Here's some simple information and additional resources for providing your kids with ways to invest their Freedom Jar money.

We've divided the information into the *Three Pillars of Wealth*:

Business   Stock Market   Real Estate

YOUR KIDS ARE LITTLE ENTREPRENEURS

Kids are full of great ideas; just like us. Often, they have more creative ideas than adults, primarily because they still believe that anything is possible. They also haven't been told for years that their ideas are stupid or a waste of time.

Start listening to your kids as they walk around their world. What are they interested in? What activities do they lose themselves in? Are they constantly suggesting that this or that would be a great idea or say things like, "Mom, why doesn't someone make a...?" or "Dad, that would work so much better if you just did..."

I'm convinced, especially after working with the kids in our camps over the years, that we are all born with the most amazing 'creative gene' and it's only through conditioning and ignorant parenting that this gene gets turned off.

So, in order not to turn it off, or to turn it back on if your child's ideas have been criticized or made fun of, start listening to him. Encourage him to think 'outside the box' in terms of what kind of a business might be viable and successful. It is also my opinion that if we're going to be starting businesses anyway, we might as well start businesses that help people and/or are environmentally friendly.

If we encourage our children to think in this way from the beginning, more and more of our future businesses will be safe for the earth and serve a grander purpose than just to sell more piddlyjunk to make money for someone.

To get started, sit down with your child and make a list of all the things he or she loves to do or is interested in:

_____

_____

_____

_____

_____

_____

_____

Now, ask these questions:

1) Is there something you could create or a service you could offer that would make (subject from your list) more enjoyable, easier to participate in, cheaper to do, etc.?

_____

_____

_____

_____

_____

_____

2) Would it be possible to turn this 'something' into a little business?
_____ Yes _____ No

3) If Yes, what would it take to turn this idea into a business?

_____

_____

_____

_____

_____

_____

_____

_____

4) Is the market (people who would buy your product or service) big enough for you to create a profitable business?

_____ Yes _____ No

5) Is someone doing something similar? _____ Yes _____ No

If the answer is NO, it might be time to start doing some research. Help your child (if he needs help) look this idea up on the internet, in the bookstore, in the phone book, through your local Chamber of Commerce.

Once he's discovered a feasible business idea, there are many steps that need to happen to actually start the business. One of the first steps is to create a business plan. For a simple Business Plan Template you can use with your child, download one here:

www.ultimateallowancebook.com/UAB/BusinessPlan.pdf

You'll find many of these steps in the books on the following page.

If you're wondering what your kids might learn from starting a business, look at this list:

Maturity • Responsibility • Dependability

Frugality • Budgeting • Financial Skills

Communication Skills • Computer Skills

Math Skills • Self-management Skills

Independence • His/Her Own Money

Self-esteem and Self-worth

Ability to Provide For Others

A Way to Give Back and Do Good in the World

To top it off, a business will give them money so they can also practice and learn how to invest money in other assets, including the stock market. All in all, this is a very good thing.

Another important concept we teach in all our programs is something we call *Financial Foursquare*. It's very similar to Robert Kiyosaki's Cash Flow Quadrant (see books below) in that it shows people how they earn or make money with regard to being an employee, self-employed (owning your own job), a business owner and an investor. An interesting distinction about how you earn money shows up in this one question:

How many times do you get paid for each hour you work?

If you only get paid once, you are *earning* money. In other words, you are trading your time and energy for it. If you are getting paid over and over again (book royalties, sales of CD/DVDs, sales on the internet of e-books, etc.), you have now crossed over into *making* money. This also is a very good thing. As long as we continue to trade our time and energy for money, getting paid per hour or on salary, we will never be truly financially free. Learning to evaluate your career choices and income generating options in terms of these distinctions, gives you a whole new outlook on working for a living.

Here are some additional resources to help your child explore and start a small business. For additional ideas, simply type the words 'entrepreneurship,' 'business' and 'kids' into any browser and you'll find tons of additional information to help you help your child step into the incredible world of entrepreneurship and building businesses.

GREAT BOOKS TO READ:
- ❏ *Cash Flow Quadrant* by Robert Kiyosaki
- ❏ *Fast Cash for Kids* by Bonnie and Noel Drew
- ❏ *Money* by New Moon
- ❏ *Realionaire* by Farrah Gray
- ❏ *The Complete Idiot's Guide to Money-Smart Kids* by Barbara Weltman.
- ❏ *The Kids' Guide To Business* by Jeff M. Brown
- ❏ *The New Totally Awesome Business Book for Kids* by Arthur Bochner & Rose Bochner.
- ❏ *The Young Entrepreneur's Guide to Starting and Running a Business* by Steve Mariotti

- ❏ *The 4-Hour Work Week* by Timothy Ferris
- ❏ *You Call the Shots* by Cameron Johnson

GREAT WEBSITES TO VISIT:
- ❏ http://www.teachingkidsbusiness.com
- ❏ http://www.WaysForKidsToEarnMoney.com
- ❏ http://www.gazillionaire.com/gaz.html
- ❏ http://www.farrahgray.com
- ❏ http://www.nfte.com/
- ❏ http://www.bizworldgame.com
- ❏ http://www.internetbasedkids.com/
- ❏ http://www.moneyinstructor.com/art/childbusiness.asp
- ❏ http://biz4kids.com
- ❏ http://www.bizworld.org
- ❏ http://www.teachingkidsbusiness.com/kidse-marketplace.htm
- ❏ http://life.familyeducation.com/money-and-kids/jobs-and-chores/48033.html
- ❏ http://www.inventorsworkshop.info
- ❏ http://www.ecitycleveland.com/index.asp

YOUR KIDS AND THE STOCK MARKET

The stock market is usually the first place people think of when the subject of investing comes up, because it's normally what people giving investment advice talk about. The stock market is a great place to start investing your kids' FREEDOM Jar dollars. Learning about the stock market, and how powerful it truly is to 'start early,' is one of the most valuable things your child can learn.

Here's how you might approach explaining the stock market to your child, if she doesn't understand it yet.

Sit down with your child and the business section of the local paper. Go to the listings for the New York Stock Exchange or the NASDAQ exchange. Find a company your child is familiar with, such as Disney, Apple, Microsoft or McDonald's. Explain that stock (referred to as shares) in a company represents a piece of ownership in the company.

146

Explain what the numbers in the paper for the stock you have selected mean.

Stock	Dividend	Last	Change
NUS	.08	25.15	+.50

NUS (Nu Skin Enterprises, Inc.) is the ticker symbol (stock's nickname); .08 is the dividend (piece of the profit); 25.15 is the last price the stock traded at before the market closed that day and +.50 is the change in the stock price (value) from the closing price the previous day. A great place to learn how to read a stock table or quote is:

http://investopedia.com/university/stocks/stocks6.asp.

Ask your child if he has any questions. Help him track the price of the stock over the next few weeks. There are several places on the web where you can help your child create an account where he can do what's called Paper Trading, i.e., pretending to buy and sell stocks and mutual funds. See a great example at:

http://finance.yahoo.com

Point out the stock tickers on CNN and CNBC. At the end of each week, review the price changes and see what other questions your child may have. If he's excited about it, continue picking more companies and watch them over time. Depending on your child, he will either find it fascinating or be bored. If he does find it's fun to research and pick stocks and watch them, then help him learn more.

There are a ton of resources to help you and your child explore the fascinating world of the stock market. For additional ideas, type the words 'investing or stock market' and 'kids' into any browser and you'll find tons of additional information to help you help your child learn about stocks and mutual funds.

If you don't understand the stock market, rest easy. Not only are there amazing books for beginners, but most financial advisors worth their salt and looking for new clients are happy to introduce people to the stock market. Simply call around or ask your friends for a referral. Let them know that you want to expose your child to the stock market and also need to learn more yourself. You can also check your local community college for a continuing education or adult education class, which is a great way to learn.

GREAT BOOKS TO READ:

❏ *Growing Money* by Gail Karlitz & Debbie Honig
❏ *Learn to Earn* by Peter Lynch
❏ *The Little Book that Beat the Market* by Joe Greenblat
❏ *The New Totally Awesome Money Book* for Kids by Arthur Bochner & Rose Bochner
❏ *Multiple Streams of Income* by Robert Allen

GREAT WEBSITES TO VISIT:

❏ http://www.investorwords.com
❏ http://library.thinkquest.org/3096/
❏ http://webtech.kennesaw.edu/jcheek3/stock_market.htm (lists tons of other websites)
❏ http://www.younginvestor.com/
❏ http://beginnersinvest.about.com/od/investingforkids/ Investing_for_Kids_and_Teens.htm
❏ http://investools.com
❏ http://buyandhold.com/bh/en/

YOUR KIDS AND REAL ESTATE

Since eight out of ten wealthy individuals in this country have made their riches in real estate or have real estate in their portfolios, it only makes sense to expose your child to the world of real estate. Many adults are afraid of investing in real estate but it's generally because they don't understand it. Again, now is a great time to learn along with your child.

Yes, it is true that you can buy real estate 'creatively,' especially in today's market, using 'owner financing' and other methods known to investors in the business such as buying property 'Subject To Existing Financing' or 'Wholesaling.' These methods of obtaining real estate allow you to possibly purchase property with little or no money down or out of pocket. It is using leverage — using other people's time, energy and money to make you money — to its fullest advantage.

Since your child's Freedom Jar may seem small initially, as it grows, you will want to help him "leverage" it as much as possible and one of the greatest forms of leverage is through real estate. For example, how much money would your child need if he wanted to buy $1000 worth of stock? Answer: $1000. But, using that same scenario, there are many ways that same $1000 could purchase a $50,000 or even a $100,000 property! Small amounts (as it may seem to you and your child) can go a long way in buying real estate creatively.

But it does not stop there. Without going into a long dissertation about real estate, understand that the same property your child purchased (with your help of course, since a child cannot sign a contract until he is 18), could also produce $100 a month or more in the form of positive cash flow (rental income minus mortgage payment, which is also referred to as the net rental income). That's $1200 a year on a $1000 investment, or a 120% return on his investment!

Keep in mind that the wealthy in this country are always 'ROI" (return on investment) minded! We call this cash flow or passive income and when kids experience making money by putting their money to work for them, all I have to say is, Watch Out!

OK, so many of you may be asking, "Where on Earth can you buy a piece of property for $50,000 these days?" The fact is there are still many markets around the country that do cash flow, do not cost a fortune and can make you money in the long run. With real estate, as with business and the stock market, investing in it takes the development of strategies and systems and it's only through education that those strategies and systems are developed.

There aren't any books for kids on real estate that I found in my resource search but there's a tremendous amount of information available on the internet and in the bookstores for adults. The Rich

---

CREATIVE WEALTH PRINCIPLE

Leverage is Using Other People's Time, Energy
and Money to Make YOU Money.

Dad series of books is a great way to start. These books are easy to read and include simple to understand examples.

GREAT BOOKS TO READ:

❏ *Real Estate Investing for Dummies* by Eric Tyson and Robert S. Griswold

❏ *The ABCs of Real Estate Investing* by Ken McElroy (Rich Dad Series)

GREAT WEBSITES TO VISIT:

❏ http://www.realtycounselors.com/real-estate-stories.html

❏ http://www.helpustohelpyou.net

OTHER FREEDOM JAR IDEAS

You can help your child start a ROTH IRA at any age. Just remember that contributions must come from *earned income*. For a great starting article on this topic, visit:

www.fairmark.com/rothira/minors.htm

One other great source for their Freedom Jar money is to purchase real estate in what is called a Self Directed IRA (which is only available through six sources nationally). Again, keeping this discussion to a minimum, let's review an example: What if your child had a Self Directed IRA account and used $100 out of it as a deposit to secure a real estate purchase. There is a process known in the real estate world as *wholesaling*, which simply means that you (on behalf of your child) could secure a real estate contract and then *assign* that contract to another buyer for more than what your contract is for.

For example, if you offer to purchase a property from a seller for $100,000 and secure (sign) a contract for that amount, you are entitled to find a buyer who is willing to pay you $110,000 for that property and you simply *assign* (sign over) your contract to him/her. That means you have just made $10,000!!! Since the $100 (deposit to secure the contract) came out of your child's Self Directed IRA, the $10,000 profit has to go back in the IRA. But, you wanted it to grow, right? There's no limit to the number of transactions you and your child can do to feed your child's IRA, or yours!

150

Lastly, to get the most leverage from a child's Freedom Jar money, you might want to investigate an IDA (Individual Development Account), offered by various banking institutions and some credit unions. An IDA is a government subsidized savings program whereby a child may open up a savings account and make regularly scheduled deposits to that account and the institution will match his deposits! Those matches could be anywhere from 1:1 up to 6:1. That's right. If your child deposits $100 into the account, it is feasible (depending on the purpose of the account and the program itself) that the institution could match that deposit with another $100 into the account and may match it up to $600! These accounts are set up for the child's education, first home, etc. You should check with each institution about their various programs. The one rule for all programs is, of course, that the money cannot be withdrawn until the goal is reached by the child and then, of course, only if it is used for the purpose it was set up to serve.

ADDITIONAL RESOURCES:

1) IDA (Individual Development Account): use Google along with your state in the search field. There are too many resources to mention.

2) Self-Directed IRA: www.pensco.com

A NOTE ABOUT ACCUMULATION VERSUS UTILIZATION

For decades, we have been conditioned to think about financial freedom and retirement in terms of *accumulating* enough money to live on when we're older.

A fresh approach and a philosophy we teach to all ages is to think in terms of creating financial freedom early by *utilizing* money in a creative way to develop passive income streams, i.e., cash flow, that allows you and your children to be financially free sooner than later.

Entrepreneurship combined with internet marketing is one of the coolest ways to develop passive income streams. And again, the two great books on this topic are *The 4-Hour Work Week* by Timothy Ferris and *Your Portable Empire* by Pat O'Bryan.

So, as you can see, there's plenty you can help your child do with his or her FREEDOM Jar money. The sheer number of options and information available to you can be overwhelming.

My suggestion is to learn about one of the *Three Pillars of Wealth* at a time. First, study the stock market together for a while. Then, learn a bit about real estate, and then, wander over to the entrepreneurial side for awhile. Most people tend to favor one or two of the pillars. Notice which one you and your child tend to enjoy the most and become an expert in that area first.

Most wealthy people have investments in all three pillars but they tend to focus on one. So, just pick one and go for it. The idea is to get your kids thinking about investing early.

CREATIVE WEALTH PRINCIPLE
Save Early, Save often, Invest Wisely

NOTES:

WHAT HAPPENS WHEN THEY START MAKING THEIR OWN MONEY?

"My formula for success? Rise early, work late, strike oil."
~ J. PAUL GETTY

Even though you are giving your child this new types of allowance, it's critical that you also encourage your child to earn extra money, when they are ready, by baby-sitting, mowing lawns, walking the neighbor's dog or starting some other form of business (lemonade stand ring a bell?). In addition, you may also wish to employ their services for jobs and projects that are outside the normal realm of household responsibilities, such as washing the family cars, helping you in the family business, taking over the responsibility of making school lunches for siblings, doing the family laundry, etc. What qualifies as an extra activity is completely up to you, and will probably involve a little pleading from them.

The age that they start earning their own money is anyone's guess. It really depends on the child. Some kids start wanting to earn 'extra cash' early, as early as 5 or 6, by offering to do extra things around the house, seeing an opportunity to start a little business that buys and sells something or provides a service for others.

On the other hand, some kids may be completely oblivious and never notice or want opportunities to make extra money. They may make it to graduation rarely earning their own money. It just depends on the kid, the situation, the neighborhood, the example you are setting, and more.

However, for that child who isn't noticing, I would strongly encourage you to do whatever you can to get him interested in making money for himself. For all kids, I encourage parents to teach them to think like a store owner or think like a banker!

Thinking like a store owner means finding a need and filling it, otherwise known as a *niche*, and there's a good reason it rhymes

153

with *rich*! Kids see these opportunities often and if you don't know how to help them start a little business, find a mentor for them who can. It's a fact that a large percentage of wealthy people have become wealthy by investing in business in one way or another. Even real estate investors usually own businesses that invest in real estate.

> *"A banker is someone who charges you high interest*
> *to borrow somebody else's money."*

Thinking like a banker means using the concept of leverage; that is, using *other people's money* (and time and energy), to make *them* money. Leveraging is one of the most important concepts we teach in camp. When you help your child start her first bank account, be sure to have her ask the banker what the bank does with her money. Point out that the bank loans it to other people and charges them more interest than it is paying on her savings account. This conversation always gets kids thinkin'! (It might just get you thinkin' as well!)

An important point here is teaching your child the concept of *"the spread."* The 'spread' isn't peanut butter, it's the difference between what you can borrow money for and what you can make by using or loaning the money out, usually in terms of the interest rate. In the bank example above, your child's savings account may earn 4% and the bank loans that out to someone who needs a car loan and charges them 10%. The spread in this situation is 6%. Not too bad. Wealthy people think about the spread all the time so let's teach our children this concept early.

 In terms of setting your children up for financial success, encouraging their entrepreneurial spirit, in my opinion, is the single most wonderful gift you can give them. One statistic I heard recently was that by the year 2015, up to 47% of Americans will be self-employed, which means they are going to have to learn and understand how to run a business, including the financial and legal aspects of business; corporate structure; trademarks, copyrights and patents; sales and marketing; accounting and more. If you're an entrepreneur yourself, you are probably already setting the example and encouraging your child to think similarly. It's amazing

what happens when you simply get their little wheels of creativity started.

Let's look at the different ways you can handle and help your child allocate the extra financial resources he or she may be making.

OPTION ONE:

You can treat extra income as bonus money and encourage your child to simply distribute this money into his Money Jars just as he would his regular allowance. In this case, you will continue to fund all his needs and activities. I don't generally recommend this method as it continues a hefty dependence on you. Our goal, remember, is to create financial independence, not dependence.

If you can afford this route and if your child is being incredibly responsible with the extra income, i.e., spending it wisely, saving up for things he wants, saving for college, starting to invest, donating regularly, etc., and you are being very diligent about the lessons he is learning, then go ahead and try this arrangement.

The lesson of putting the extra earned income into assets so that he starts to earn residual or passive income is especially valuable in this case. An example may be to start a college fund (for example, a 529 plan) that is invested in mutual funds, index funds, ETFs (exchange traded funds) or even individual stocks if you have someone to guide you in this arena. Don't forget to help your child start and contribute to his ROTH IRA also.

OPTION TWO:

You and your child can deduct part or all of the extra earned income from his total allowance amount. As he gets older, the amount you put toward his needs and wants decreases and the amount he contributes increases. Again, the amounts are totally arbitrary and up to you and your child. You may have him contribute any percentage that you both agree on, toward his allowance amount, as much as half of his earnings or as little as 10%. I wouldn't necessarily put all of his money toward covering his own expenses until perhaps his later teen years.

Remember, regardless of the amount he is required to contribute toward his own care (needs and wants), he is still utilizing his Money Jars at all times.

HERE'S A SUGGESTION:

If your child is going to go to college, you can lengthen the time before your child takes over all of his or her own expenses. If your child probably won't be going to college, you'll want to make sure he is fully responsible by the time he leaves home or graduates from high school. I think it's important, since such a huge percentage of kids never even make it to college, that all kids know that college is just one road they can take to success, not the *only* road. I think it's a disservice for our society to make a teen think that he is a failure right off the bat because he chooses not to go, or can't afford to go, to college.

NOTE: Remember that children much prefer spending your money instead of theirs so you will probably get some resistance to Option Two, at first. However, simply explain that the goal is to make him fully responsible for himself by the time he leaves home, and that requires that he begin taking increasing responsibility for his own financial well-being as he gets older.

Just as in life, there are exceptions for every rule and especially for rules of thumb. Let's say your daughter wants to save up for a very special purchase, maybe a special breed of puppy, a special trip with a friend, a new saddle for her horse or a musical instrument; something that's going to take some time to save up for. You may want to make an exception to her contribution percentage for that period of time so that she can save for this item or event. It's a wonderful opportunity for her to experience a great success around saving to buy the things she wants.

When helping your child be successful saving for something he or she really wants, it's a great time to explain the dangers of using credit cards to buy things when you don't have the cash to pay for them. Showing a child how compound interest works *against* them can be a real eye-opener and getting them used to saving to buy the things they want is a valuable lesson that even VISA would say is priceless!

You can use the simple worksheet and formula on the next page to help your child plan and save up for a purchase.

SAVING FOR PURCHASE WORKSHEET—EXAMPLE

Current Date	Item	Cost of Item	Months to Save	Amount to Save	Projected Purchase Date
1/1/07	Saddle	$500	6	$85	July 1, 2007

AMOUNT TO SAVE =

COST OF ITEM DIVIDED BY MONTHS TO SAVE OR 500/6 = $85

OK, it's your turn:

SAVING FOR PURCHASE WORKSHEET

Current Date	Item	Cost of Item	Months to Save	Amount to Save	Projected Purchase Date

AMOUNT TO SAVE =

COST OF ITEM DIVIDED BY MONTHS TO SAVE OR

_____/_____= _____

THE CREDIT CARD QUESTION:
SHOULD YOU OR SHOULDN'T YOU?

"Creditors have better memories than debtors."
~ BENJAMIN FRANKLIN

My initial gut reaction to this question is **NO,** you should not get your teenager a credit card! But, after considering all the facts, and the reality of our current financial paradigm, it might not be such a bad idea IF there is a strong foundation of education and experience put into place first.

Some say getting a teenager a credit card will help him learn to be financially responsible, but many times it's a recipe for financial disaster. Give them plastic, yes. But in the form of a debit card, not a credit card. They must learn to manage their *own* money before they begin messing around with other people's money.

Teens are now the most heavily targeted age group in terms of advertising campaigns because they have so much disposable income available. There are entire seminars designed to teach companies how to market to teens. The pressure of being cool, doing the things the other kids do and having the things the other kids have, creates the potential for a financial mess.

I still remember the day I got my first VISA card. I bought a stuffed black and white striped cat and named him VISA! No kidding! (I'm pretty sure that cat is still in my garage in a box! Talk about piddlyjunk.)

The usual justification for teens or college students having a credit card is that they need it to start their credit history and begin to establish their credit score. I say there is plenty of time to establish a credit history after college, if they are going to college. Back when we didn't get

159

credit cards until we were 20 or older, none of us had trouble buying our first car, and few of us were ready to buy our first piece of real estate at that time (though I'd like to change this). The fact is, most teens and college student, *generally* don't have the maturity it takes to use credit cards wisely. After all, just look at the number of *mature* adults who don't!

CREATIVE WEALTH PRINCIPLE

If You Can't Afford It In Cash, You Can't Afford It At All.

Why put your kids in a situation where they may be tempted to buy something they don't need and have to pay for it, literally, for years? You may well ask, "But how can I control what my teen does when he goes off to college? He doesn't need my approval to get a credit card."

You're absolutely correct; he doesn't. But are you helping your son or daughter with school? If you are, then tell him that he is not allowed to get a credit card as long as you are helping him pay for school. If he gets a card, you will stop helping. Period. And mean it. It's not about being mean; it's about being the parent and knowing what's best for your child.

Are there teens and college students that can handle using a credit card wisely? Sure there are. But unless you know without a shadow of a doubt that your son or daughter is one of these kids, you're playing with fire. Have *you* ever used your credit card unwisely, wishing you hadn't bought this or that with someone else's money? I know I have and I'm a very responsible, knowledgeable, mature adult. For the most part, teens and young college students aren't (yet) and all the statistics prove it.

Use page 182 to show your kids how credit cards can hurt them if they don't learn to use them properly.

I have a surprise for you! Since I wanted to give you the best advice available in terms of how, and what, to teach your kids about credit, debt and credit cards, I went right to the source. Curtis Arnold is the founder of CardRatings.com and the author of *How to Profit From Credit Cards*. He has some words for you. Read on...

CREDIT, DEBT AND PLASTIC MONSTERS: WHAT YOUR KIDS NEED TO SUCCEED

© 2008 Curtis E. Arnold

Unless you've shopped for a toddler lately, you may not realize that many toys geared to children as young as three now accept pretend credit cards as well as cash. I've actually heard one toy say "Credit approved!" over and over again. Just the message we want our youngsters to hear—not!

Far too many of the 25,000 or so commercials children see on TV every year include high pressure sales pitches with toll-free numbers for credit card orders – to say nothing of the basic message—to buy, buy, buy! And now, our little ones are going online, where paying with plastic is par for the course.

Children learn young that credit cards are an easy, quick way to buy things – but they don't necessarily understand that those little pieces of plastic represent real money that we work hard to earn. And they certainly have no idea about the connection between the plastic, the bills and their parents' all-important credit reports and credit scores, which are formulas lenders use to rate our credit worthiness.

Once they leave home for college or work, your kids will be bombarded with credit card offers. Ideally, by that time, your children will have learned about the relationship between credit and debt and will have had many positive credit experiences, thanks to your good example. Even if your example hasn't been so good, you can begin, even before they go to kindergarten, to speak honestly about the pros and cons of credit and debt.

HOW TO TALK ABOUT CREDIT AND DEBT WITH CHILDREN

Look for opportunities to discuss credit when your children are pre-schoolers. For example, when you're playing "pretend" store, explain why you don't want to charge your purchases—because credit cards can make it too easy and too expensive to buy things you don't need or really, really want.

In your give and take with the young shopkeepers, discuss what happens when you can't afford the "piddlyjunk" (as Elisabeth would put it) you buy with a credit card. Make clear that when you can't pay the credit card bill on time, you'll have to pay even more.

As an example, play "Pet Store" using all of the household's stuffed animals (this can be quite a zoo if you have several young ones!). Buy one with your credit card and tell your young shop owner to send you a bill. When they give you the bill, tell them you don't have enough money to pay them in full. Make a partial payment (with play money) and ask your shopkeeper to send you a second bill, adding in the interest because you didn't pay the first bill in full.

For a more realistic role-playing scenario, bring in a child or adult to serve as the credit card company who gives the store owner the money for the stuffed animal and have the credit card company send you the bill. Use play money to really illustrate the point, and if your child is highly visual, illustrate the transaction on paper.

Tell your child, "Every time we use our credit cards, we're really getting a loan from the bank or credit card company, which quickly pays the store for what we charged on the credit card. If we don't pay the bank or credit card company right back, we have to pay extra money, called interest, which doesn't buy anything new. It just makes the things we've already bought more expensive. Interest is like a rental fee that the bank charges you for using their money."

NOTE: Again, this is a great place for role-playing. Get some play money, a couple of things you've purchased recently and two big boxes with signs saying 'store' and 'credit card company/bank'. Actually walk your kids through the scenario of how the money changes hands.

Here's an example you can use with teens using real numbers: If you owe $10,000 on a typical credit card that charges 18% interest and you only send in the required minimum payments, you'll spend $38,930.64 before you pay it off completely, assuming you don't charge another penny to the card or pay any fees over the 57 years it will take to pay off the balance, by which time your children may be taking care of you! (**NOTE**: minimum payment was calculated based on 2% of the balance.)

While there's no benefit to going into all these numbers with a toddler (unless you happen to have a math prodigy), children just a little older will understand the basics. Grade schoolers hear about credit cards all the time and can understand the concept of paying for the privilege of borrowing money, a.k.a. interest. It's very important that they grasp how that interest can double, triple, or even quadruple the amount owed, leaving two, three, or four times less for other things.

As they age, your children will be exposed to yet more opportunities to spend, and unfortunately, credit card companies are targeting pre-teens now. So it's important that young children know about credit and debt at an even younger age than you'd like. Hopefully, you are carefully budgeting your money, paying off your debts and avoiding any of the "triggers" that get you to overspend. But even if you haven't set the best example, go over a few credit card bills with your pre-teen.

Then, I suggest that you sit down at the computer together, and surf on over to the online calculator section of CardRatings.com, the card comparison site that I founded. Plug in the numbers for one of your credit card bills and take a look at how much it would cost to pay off what you owe if you only send in the minimums. Discuss what else you might do with that money (for example, investing it instead!). If your kid's anything like my own, he or she will have lots of ideas!

It is also a good idea to locate this card on your credit report. (If you don't have a current copy, go to AnnualCreditReport.com to order your free reports.) As you look it over with your child, discuss how a report card is like a credit report and why it's important to get homework in on time. "The better your report card, the better your chances of getting into a great college and/or earning a good salary." (Note from the author. Please remember that not all kids end up going to college, nor is college an indicator of success in life, financially or otherwise. Many very wealthy individuals either never went to, or didn't finish, college.)

Credit basics are the same. One way to get great credit reports and scores is to always pay bills on time and never spend more than you can afford. The better your credit report and the higher your credit score, the better your chances are of getting a great deal on such things as credit cards, car loans and mortgages. Landlords, employers and insurance companies also base decisions on credit reports.

Discuss the tempting credit card offers you get in the mail or see online with your children. Remember, if it sounds too good to be true, it probably is! Visit CardRatings.com and see my new book, *How to Profit from Credit Cards: Using Credit to Improve Your Financial Life and Bottom Line* (FT Press, 2008) for advice on figuring out which cards are best for you.

TEACHING TEENS ABOUT CREDIT

The older kids are, the more they can understand and appreciate:

- The messages sent by advertisers and card issuers that are designed to get them to spend.

- The difference between wants and needs.

- The lure of "buy now/pay later."

- The peer pressure trap.

By the time your teens enter high school, it's crucial that they can separate out the marketing messages related to the incredibly tempting card offers they're about to get, if they're not receiving offers already.

Watch out! Card issuers know how much money we spend on our teens and how much of their own money they spend. High school students are still a relatively untapped market ("unserved" in lender lingo) and issuers are going after this market with "prepaid teen cards," some of which accept 13-year-olds.

In response, we have to "double-down" on our efforts to teach teens the importance of budgeting and making conscious choices about spending, borrowing and saving. Aside from implementing Elisabeth's effective *Ultimate Allowance System* in this book, I recommend:

www.CreditCardNation.com

The site belongs to Dr. Robert D. Manning, author of *Credit Card Nation* (Basic Books, 2001). Take his financial literacy quiz with your teen and check out his budget estimator, which offers average salaries for various careers. Play around with the numbers and let your teen try to make ends meet.

The Jump$tart Coalition for personal financial literacy, which has an online database (JumpStart.org) for parents and students interested in learning more about personal finance, including credit matters.

SO, SHOULD YOUR TEENAGER GET A CREDIT CARD?

I see valid arguments on both sides of this issue. While I'd never advocate a card for every teen, there's security in knowing that your teen has a back up solution for emergencies. Also, believe it or not, using a credit card is safer than using cash and can offer more consumer protection than a debit card. If your teen's credit card is lost or stolen, chances are there'll be zero liability for unauthorized charges. But, most important, in my humble opinion, your child will have had experience with credit cards and all of their hidden traps, before they're deluged with the "No credit check, no co-signer or no income" offers if, and when, they reach college. Ultimately, though, there is no black and white answer to this question. I think a lot depends on individual circumstances.

There are now many prepaid cards geared to pre-college teens (teens normally aren't legally allowed to get a credit card in their own name until they're 18). Visa's Buxx card, for example, is promoted as being parent-controlled, re-loadable and a great way to teach budgeting and money management to teens. When it first came on the market in 2001, the Buxx card sparked a great deal of discussion. Now, there are several versions of this type of card, with a variety of enrollment and reloading fees.

Don't be surprised if you're soon pressured to get one by your teen! These cards are marketed to them as cool status symbols that make it easier to get the latest "must-have" stuff. The best of them offer online tools designed to help parents teach their youngsters about money, credit and debt. Some also try to motivate high school students to learn more about managing money.

Unfortunately, many focus mainly on encouraging teen spending and only give the education component lip service. Elisabeth's opinion to teach children to use their own hard-earned money has a lot of merit. After all, if they don't understand how to use their own money, how are we going to expect them to learn to use other people's money?

Many parents are attracted by the convenience of these cards, which can eliminate much of the need to give cash to their teens—meaning they'll be spared numerous trips to the ATM and bank. I can also see them being of some benefit to parents who want to modify Elisabeth's advice and use a card for some of the money being spent THROUGH their kids, not just ON them.

Another plus is that prepaid cards are a lot less risky than typical credit cards where you're the one whose credit will take a nose-dive if your child does something irresponsible with your card, like taking out a huge cash advance. With a prepaid card, there's only so much your teen can spend (the amount that is loaded on the card).

Unfortunately, most prepaid cards come with all sorts of fees that really add up. So, while I'm all for teens getting some real experience with plastic before they leave home, the current prepaid teen cards leave much to be desired. I'll bet better teen cards will be marketed soon, but in the meantime, you have other options that can save on the fees associated with teen cards.

For example, you can get a low-limit credit card and let your teen be an authorized user. The downside is that your credit rating is the one that will be on the line because you'll be the primary account holder. If you choose this option, make sure you limit your risk by asking for a very low limit on the card, such as $200 or $300. One upside to this option is that this technique may help your teen start to establish a credit history as some card issuers report authorized users to one or more of the three major credit bureaus.

The final, and best, option is to get your teen a debit card (a.k.a. check card), in order to give him instant access to his own money in his own checking account, not money borrowed from a card issuer. One potential drawback (albeit rare) is that instant access means a thief can spend all the money in a checking account in minutes, leading to bounced checks, overdraft fees and a major headache. But again, what a great lesson this can be for your child in terms of using his debit card wisely and safely, painful as an experience like this may be at the time.

If you're going to allow your kids to use debit cards, make sure to find out the bank's policies on debit card liability. If your child's account is exposed to fraudsters, it will typically take hours to straighten things out, including credit reports and scores, even if all the money's returned and the fees reversed. Again, not a bad thing if there are major lessons to be learned by all.

I've toyed with the notion of using all three of these types of cards with my own teenager. But when it comes right down to it, I don't think most youngsters really "get" that plastic in any form is real money. While it's a little more inconvenient, I pay kids in cash or by check for jobs well done, as well as for allowances. The only plastic I have given our oldest teen is a "plain jane" ATM card (that doesn't double as a debit card). It makes spending and budgeting decisions much more concrete. When there's no more left, they're out of luck and it's time for Plan B, which is a great time to sit them down and talk a bit more about money, credit and budgeting, not to mention how to make more of the green stuff.

HOW TO MAKE SURE YOUR TEEN'S FIRST CARD IS A GOOD EXPERIENCE

Discuss the rules about how and when the card can be used. If only for emergencies, share this definition: "If you can eat it, drink it or wear it, it's not an emergency!" That's what David Hunt, former president of AT&T Universal Card, said when he gave his daughter a credit card as she went off to college.

Make sure your teen knows what the consequences will be if he can't pay the bill in full, every month. Will you bail him out, or will he be on his own?

Visit CardRatings.com together and look over the student credit card offerings with no annual fees.

Discuss interest rates (avoid a rate in the high teens like the plague), cash advances, fees, due dates and grace periods. If you want a refresher on these terms as well as help with analyzing the various offers, consider getting my book, *How to Profit from Credit Cards*.

Apply for the card you both choose, again discussing the family's rules and what's at stake if your credit report is harmed.

Go over the credit card statement every single month with your teen, discussing what he will pay in interest, fees and penalties if the bill isn't paid in full and on time, every month. Discuss each purchase, whether it was a want or need, whether or not it could have waited, etc.

Make sure the bill is paid on time and in full every month. Enforce your rules!

WHAT TO TELL COLLEGE STUDENTS

I often speak on college campuses, and here's what I tell the students:

"I know first-hand about the dangers of getting into credit card debt while you're in school. Before I turned my life around, I had $45,000 in credit card debt and was under unbelievable stress. You probably have a credit card already, and if not, you will likely get one soon. Certainly, if lenders get their way, you'll have a pile in your pocket by the time you graduate!"

"Three out of every four college students had at least one card in 2004, with the average freshman balance at $1,585, while many students maxed out their cards entirely, according to Nellie Mae, the largest nonprofit provider of student loans. The typical undergrad card balance was $2,169, although newer estimates put it closer to $3,000. According to a recent poll, one in four college students has two to three credit cards, and nearly one-third say it's difficult to keep up with expenses because they're already in debt."

"Card issuers spend millions each year aggressively marketing on campuses because they want to develop long-term financial relationships with you. Here are my tips for making the most of the situation:

- Compare offers by reading the terms and conditions carefully. Choose the best card for you, regardless of the freebies. Ask for a low credit limit (around $500) so you won't be tempted to charge more than you should, and steer clear of reward cards until you know you can use credit responsibly. (Studies show we charge more with them.)

- Always pay your bills on time. Not to do so means you'll pay fees and a higher interest rate, potentially on all your debts. A spreadsheet can keep you organized and on time with your payments. If you think you might forget, consider signing up for automatic bill-paying.

- Always pay off your balance. The first month you don't, stop using your cards immediately! Use only cash or a debt card until you're sure you'll use your cards responsibly.

- Don't use your card as a source of income. Take it from me, I know firsthand how devastating this can be. Credit is a privilege, and it's your responsibility to make sure it doesn't become a peril and ruin your credit reports and credit scores.

- Keep out of the malls, avoid impulse buying and focus on free activities. Join campus organizations, volunteer for local nonprofits, take a hike, or you can always get a job.

- Take a personal finance course as soon as possible. What you learn will be more important and practical for your future than what's covered in most classrooms. Also, stay on top of credit news, so you'll be aware of industry practices. For example, lately, banks have been lowering people's credit limits.

- Already in debt? Stop charging and always pay more than the minimum. If you're carrying a balance on more than one card, you'll save the most if you pay off the one with the highest rate first, then go to the next highest interest card, and so on. Pay the

169

minimum on all cards but the one with the highest interest. Pay it off and start on the next one.

- Get help if you're buried in debt. Not facing financial problems doesn't make them go away. Talk to your family, a clergy member, a credit counselor (NFCC.org lists reputable counselors), someone on campus—anyone you trust who can help you figure things out."

Don't worry! Since you've already educated your kids about credit and debt, you won't have to worry about problems like this when they're out on their own or off to college, right? We can only hope.

To sum things up, giving credit to teens can be a double-edged sword. If handled properly (a good dose of parental involvement goes a long way), credit can really empower your teen and help him establish a firm financial footing.

On the flip side, improper use can have a devastating financial impact on your teen and scar him or her for many years to come. Given the importance of credit scores in our society today (a bad score can even prevent your teen from getting a job), I implore you to take the initiative and help your teen develop positive credit habits. If you don't, I can assure you your teen will likely be fighting a losing battle...one that all too often has deadly consequences.*

Good luck. You can do it!

Curtis E. Arnold is the CEO/Founder of CardRatings.com and is an expert on credit. He is also the author of *How to Profit from Credit Cards: Using Credit to Improve Your Financial Life and Bottom Line* (FT Press, 2008) and The Complete Idiot's Guide to Person-to-Person Lending (Penguin Group USA, April 2009).

*There have been several reports that college students have actually committed suicide over their credit card debt.

NOTE: To learn more about credit scores, what goes into them and how important they are, go here:

www.myfico.com/crediteducation/brochures.aspx

WHAT ELSE DO THEY NEED TO KNOW?

This book introduces several important concepts your children need to know in order to be financially successful in life. However, there is a lot more for them to learn:

- Understanding the difference between *assets* and *liabilities*; assets put money IN your pocket and liabilities take money OUT of your pocket.

- Understanding the difference between *earned income* and *passive income*; earned income is money you trade your time and energy for and passive income is income that comes in with little or no work after awhile. Passive income is the key to financial freedom.

- Understanding a concept we teach in our programs called Financial Foursquare™. Whether your child earns money as an employee, is self-employed, or owns a business, he must also be an investor.

- Understanding how to put their money to work for them.

- Understanding how to use OPM (other people's money) and the power of leverage to make them money.

- Understanding compound interest and compound growth and its amazing role in making money grow.

- Understanding the difference between good debt and bad debt.

- Understanding the powerful tools successful people use to set and achieve their goals.

- Understanding the power behind their thoughts, beliefs and attitudes about everything.

- A basic understanding of economy.

- Understanding how to use credit wisely and the dangers of abusing it.

- Understanding the importance of investing in all Three Pillars of Wealth (stocks, real estate and business) and how regular, everyday people use leverage to become wealthy.

Those concepts are just a few of the many wealth principles we teach in our *Creative Cash for Kids and Creative Cash at School* programs and in our unique *Camp Millionaire, Moving Out! for Teens, Creative Wealth Intensive and Creative Wealth for Women* programs.

For more information, please visit our web site at:

www.creativewealthintl.org

THE MORAL OF THE STORY

*"The perfecting of one's self is the fundamental base
of all progress and all moral development."*
~ CONFUCIUS

I urge you to remember that you're not raising children; you're raising adults. And kids need to learn certain things about life in order to make wise choices as adults. It's your job to teach them these things before they move out so they can stay out successfully.

There is a cost for acting, and there is a cost for not acting. Not preparing your child to manage and invest his or her money wisely will cost your children years of financial stress and affect their families and communities as well. It may also cost you money in the future if you have to, or choose to, rescue them financially.

By empowering your kids with the knowledge, skills and experience they need to make wise choices—financial and otherwise—you will have done all you can to prepare them to live happily, whatever that ends up meaning to them.

One of the most valuable things my parents taught me was the concept of being resourceful. They don't need to know everything; they just need to know where to find everything!

The other valuable lesson my Mother instilled in me was that I could do anything I set my mind to.

Teaching your child that anything is possible is a lesson that will last forever. If you can instill this mind-set in your children, you're giving them the biggest gift of all. Napoleon Hill, author of *Think and Grow Rich*, once said:

"What the mind can conceive and believe, the mind can achieve."

My goals for this book were to give you tools, support and knowledge, and finally, to provide you with an allowance system that really works. I've done my part.

Now it's your turn to take this information and put it into action. Intention without action does nothing. Goals without deadlines are just dreams. By dreaming that one day you would be sending your child out into this big, wonderful world we have the awesome privilege to live in, you found this book. It is my request that you take this material and finish the job. It may be frustrating at times. It may be hard to stick with the system at times. You may think it's downright impossible sometimes, but stick with it. Your child's future, and possibly the very future of this country, depends on it. Only wise, fiscally responsible leaders will make this country strong again. There's a good chance that your properly empowered and financially prepared child may be one of them!

AND, IF YOU'D LIKE, WE OFFER THE FOLLOWING:

- Private programs (class reunions, family gatherings, corporate meetings, employees, employee's children).

- Presentations (group meetings, employee gatherings, educational, entertainment, parent meetings).

- Conferences (financial, network-marketing, parenting, education, homeschool, curriculum).

- Panels, interviews and more.

Good luck. Call or email me if you have questions!

(805) 957-1024 • (800) 928-1932

elisabeth@creativewealthintl.org

More On Money Personalities

The following information on money personalities was taken from Olivia Mellan's book, *Money Harmony: Resolving Money Conflicts in Your Life and Relationships*, Walker and Company, NY, 1995. This information included by permission from Olivia Mellan, President, Olivia Mellan and Associates, Inc.

To learn about Mellan's other books, teleclasses, audio CD, and talks, visit her web site:

www.moneyharmony.com

Remember, most of us are a mixture of the following money personality types. Our personality types can change over time. Also, couples may balance each other out.

HOARDERS

- Enjoy saving for a rainy day

- Have difficulty spending money on luxury items or immediate pleasures (entertainment, vacations, clothes)

- Like to budget and periodically review

- Assume: Money = Security

- Weakness: May be too anxious, stingy or worried to enjoy money in the moment

SPENDERS

- Enjoy buying goods and services for immediate pleasure

- Have difficulty saving money and prioritizing needs

- Feel claustrophobic when dealing with budgets

- Assume: Money = Happiness

- Weakness: May save too little and lack long-term financial security

- In extreme cases develop spending addictions

- Weakness: May experience an emotional backlash of anger—an "inner tantrum"—when curbing their spending

BINGERS

- Are a combination of hoarders and spenders

- Save and save—then blow money all at once

- Weakness: May lack long-term financial security or have relationship problems resulting from erratic behavior

MONEY MONKS

- Believe money is dirty or bad and too much of it will corrupt them

- Uncomfortable with wealth, fear you'd "sell out" or lose sight of human, political, or spiritual ideals

- Assume: money is root of all evil

- Weaknesses: May sabotage opportunities for greater financial comfort, won't "indulge" themselves or spend on life's luxuries

AVOIDERS

- Tend to avoid the various tasks of everyday money management: don't balance checkbook, don't know how much they owe or spend, and are likely to pay bills late

- May feel overwhelmed or incompetent with money management tasks, or "above" the boring details of money management

- Assume: Money is too complicated, or money is too mundane

- Weaknesses: Inability to address financial issues leads to financial mistakes and lack of long-term financial security

AMASSERS

- Are happiest when they have large amounts of money at their disposal to spend, save, or invest

- Like to make money and display money

- Assume: Money = Self-Worth or Money = Power

- Weakness: Lack of money may lead to feelings of failure. May not enjoy life, but be preoccupied with money

WORRIERS

- Worry about money all the time—what could go wrong regarding money or that would require money

- Spend a great deal of time balancing and rebalancing their checkbooks

- Probably think if they had more money they wouldn't worry, but then they'd actually worry more

- Assume: Money = Security

- Weakness: Are often miserable, and waste life obsessing over money

Some fun websites on money personalities you may want to explore with your kids:

- www.sorted.org.nz/calculators/kids-money-quiz/page1.php
- www.kathleengurney.com/news_articles/understanding-money-personalities.html
- www.financialtip.blogspot.com/2007/03/what-is-your-money-personality.html
- www.tennesseesaves.org/TeachingTools/colorofmoney/checksheet.pdf
- www.debtsmart.com/pages/article_compatibility_test.html
- www.buttebusiness.org/uploads/Money_Personality.doc

COMPOUND INTEREST

The cool part about compound interest is that as your money earns interest, that interest is added to the original amount of money you invested and IT earns interest, too. Now this is getting interesting!

YEAR	PRINCIPAL	INTEREST (7%)	ENDING BALANCE
1	$100.00	$7.00	$107.00
2	$107.00	$7.49	$114.49
3	$114.49	$8.01	$122.50
4	$122.50	$8.58	$131.08
5	$131.08	$9.18	$140.26
TOTAL INTEREST		$40.26	

The whole idea of money growing is an interesting one. Your child may ask, "Why does money grow?"

Here's a great response to the question:

"When you borrow a video from a video store, does the store owner charge you to watch it? (Yes.) Why? (Because I'm using his property.) Exactly and when you let people use your *money*, you charge them to use it!"

COMPOUND GROWTH   The same growth happens with a mutual fund, but in a slightly different way. Most mutual funds allow you to reinvest your dividends (company profits that are given out to shareholders) back into purchasing additional shares of the mutual fund. In this case, the growth is referred to as 'compound growth' because the 'growth' in the value of your account is not interest.

HOW $1 GROWS OVER TIME

GROWTH RATES (COMPOUND INTEREST RATE)

YEARS	3%	5%	7%	9%	11%	15%
1	1.03	1.05	1.07	1.09	1.11	1.15
5	1.16	1.28	1.40	1.54	1.69	2.01
10	1.34	1.63	1.97	2.37	2.64	4.05
15	1.56	2.08	2.76	3.64	4.78	8.14
20	1.81	2.65	3.87	5.60	8.06	16.37
25	2.09	3.39	5.43	8.62	13.59	32.92
30	2.43	4.32	7.61	13.27	22.89	66.21
35	2.81	5.52	10.68	20.41	38.57	133.18
40	3.26	7.04	14.97	31.41	65.00	267.86
45	3.78	8.99	21.00	48.33	109.56	538.77
50	4.38	11.46	29.46	74.36	184.56	1083.66

Keep in mind that interest rates are NEVER stable but are averaged over a period of time.

"Compounding is the 8th wonder of the world."

~ ALBERT EINSTEIN

Final Quiz

You may choose one of the options below.

CHOICE A:

Receive $25,000 today

or

CHOICE B:

Receive a single penny,
doubled every day for 30 days

My choice is:

A   or   B

Why did you make that choice?

_____

The answer is on page 215.

STEREO SCENARIO:

WHAT CREDIT CARDS REALLY COST!

(i.e., What it costs to RENT money)

Let's say you decide you want to buy a new stereo which costs $1000. You find the one you want and decide to charge the amount on your credit card instead of paying cash for it. When you get the bill, you have two choices:

1. PAY IT OFF COMPLETELY WITH MONEY IN YOUR SAVINGS ACCOUNT, IF YOU HAVE SAVED UP FOR IT, OR;

2. MAKE MONTHLY PAYMENTS UNTIL IT'S PAID OFF.

This is what you'd end up paying for the stereo (original cost of $1000) if you didn't use that card again and only made the minimum payment of $20 each month (at 18% interest) AND it would take you 19.3 years to pay this off!

$2931.00!!! - OUCH

How much extra did you pay when you charged it on a credit card and only make the minimum payment (many people do this)?_____

THE TOP 10 MONEY SCRIPTS THAT MESS UP PEOPLE'S LIVES

This information comes courtesy of Ted Klontz, Ph.D., Brad Klontz, Psy.D. and Rick Kahler, CFP, authors of the great new book, *The Financial Wisdom of Ebenezer Scrooge: 5 Principles to Transform Your Relationship with Money*. This information provided by permission.

All of our financial behaviors, even the most self-defeating, self-destructive, illogical, "I should know better," craziest ones make perfect sense when we discover the underlying *Money Script(s)* that drive them. These money scripts are at the core of all of our financial behaviors, both good and not so good. They are the internalized and typically unconscious beliefs we have about what money is, what it is not, what it can or cannot do, the role we play in it, and the role it plays in our lives. Money scripts are formed in childhood and are reinforced by our experiences throughout our lives, often appearing as self-fulfilling prophecies. Money scripts will always influence our financial beliefs and behaviors and thus every aspect of our lives until we die. Then, amazingly, they will continue to affect those who knew us who are left behind. It is essential to identify and modify these erroneous money scripts if we are to reach our financial potential or change our self- defeating and self-destructive financial behaviors.

Every money script has an element of truth in it. Not the whole truth, mind you, but an element of truth. For example while the script, "Flying is dangerous," is partially true; it is not the whole truth. Other parts of the truth are missing, such as, "Flying is safer than being a pedestrian in a major city;" "Flying is safer than riding a bicycle;" "Flying is safer than traveling by car," etc. Money scripts work the same way. While they represent a part of the truth about money, they typically do not represent the whole picture. Operating as if they are the complete and absolute truth, without regard to context, can be disastrous.

What follows are 10 of the most common money scripts that show up in our work with clients. If left unexamined and unchanged, these money scripts will contribute to some of the most common self-destructive and limiting financial behaviors that people experience.

1. MORE MONEY WILL MAKE THINGS BETTER

This money script is perhaps the most common one afflicting Americans. The problem is, when the arbitrary "more money" target is met, the peace, security, happiness, or whatever else we believe "more money" will give us never quite seems to show up. So we look for more money. Like the carrot just out of the reach of the donkey, though we are running like crazy, we never quite reach it. Entire lives, even generations of lives, can be dedicated to the pursuit of the fulfillment of this money script. The fact is, recent research suggests what so many people already intuitively know. There is no correlation between money and happiness beyond a household income of $50,000 per year, which happens to approximate the national average annual income in the U.S. In the past 100 years, affluence in the U.S. has exploded! However, there has been no significant change in our rates of depression and misery. Folks, more money, in and of itself, will NOT make things better. Unless you are living in poverty and cannot take care of your essential needs (e.g. food, clothing, shelter, etc.), happiness is NOT about the amount of money you have. There is a saying: "Wherever you go, there you are." This saying certainly applies to your financial net worth. If you are miserable at your current income level, more likely than not, you will be miserable with more money!

2. MONEY IS BAD

As with all money scripts, there are many variations to the "Money Is Bad" money script. They include such beliefs as: "The rich are shallow or greedy or insensitive or unhappy;" "The rich got that way by taking advantage of others;" "When money walks in the front door, love walks out the back door," and so on. When we operate from this unconscious money script, we are very likely to unwittingly sabotage any potential financial progress. If having money, or being rich, makes us a bad person, or will make us an unhappy person, or cause our loved ones to become distant, why would we act to accumulate any? While the truth is that some wealthy people took advantage of others to become wealthy, others were just at the right place at the right time. While still others were willing to follow a dream, a passion, or a vision and it came true for them. There are people who are wealthy and unhappy. There are people who are wealthy and very happy. There are people who are wealthy and have extraordinarily intimate loving relationships. The point is: money is neither good nor bad in and of itself; it is our own relationship to it that determines our good or bad experiences with it.

3. I DON'T DESERVE MONEY

We see this money script in many people who have money that they did not earn, or do not fully accept as their own. We see this one also in people who believe that they should not enjoy what money can give them, because others are not so fortunate. Often the "I don't deserve money" money script is associated with lower self-esteem, and keeps people emotionally and spiritually poor, despite any wealth they may have. This is also a predominant script for those who work in the helping professions. Those of us with this money script tend to be underemployed and/or make ill-advised financial decisions in an unconscious attempt to "get rid of what we don't deserve." It is a well established fact that individuals who experience "sudden money" events (e.g. lottery winners, life insurance settlements, a sale of property, sudden fame and fortune) are often back to their original level of financial existence within several years.

4. I DESERVE TO SPEND MONEY

Like all money scripts, there is always at least a grain of truth in this one. In fact, we hope you believe that you deserve to spend money on yourself and those close to you. However, believing that you deserve something extravagant, or that you need to buy something out of your price range as a gift to others at the expense of saving for your future can undermine you and your family's financial health. A related money script is one that says, "I might as well enjoy the money while I have it; if I don't, someone will come along and take it from me."

5. THERE WILL NEVER BE ENOUGH MONEY

Ebenezer Scrooge, when we first meet him in Dickens' *The Christmas Carol,* is a classic example of where this money script can take someone. When we believe there will never be enough money, we set ourselves up to live a life of deprivation, experience constant anxiety, insecurity and fear. Workaholics who sacrifice marriages, children and health, often operate from this money script. Those who grew-up in poverty, or whose family experienced poverty in previous generations, can internalize this money script. While this belief might have served us by giving us drive, ambition and a solid work ethic, it is not the whole truth, and if left unexamined, will spoil any benefits we could receive from our hard work.

6. THERE WILL ALWAYS BE ENOUGH MONEY

This money script drives the behaviors of many who grew up in wealthy families, where wants, desires and activities were not restricted by a lack of money. This script could also have its origin in families that didn't have much. In those families it may have seemed that things just showed up when they needed them. Still others may internalize this money script when they believe that others will take care of them. With this money script, an unconscious trust that the universe will always take care of us regardless of our actions or inactions is internalized. The problem arises when there is some kind of change in our universe related to our financial status. If we are not conscious of this money script, a change in our financial landscape, without changes in our beliefs and behaviors, can lead to financial disaster.

7. MONEY IS UNIMPORTANT

This money script can arise from an interpretation of certain social or religious tenets or from the money script that wealth does not bring happiness, love or belonging. However, these money scripts allow us to rationalize poor financial planning, lack of concern about financial matters, lack of ambition and sometimes even laziness. The fact is: money does have importance. It is a valuable resource that is as important as other resources in our lives, such as time, careers, relationships and health.

8. MONEY WILL GIVE ME MEANING

There is a saying: "You can never get enough of what you don't need to make you happy." Money cannot give you what it does not possess: personal meaning, happiness, fulfillment, peace, fulfilling intimate relationships, a sense of belonging, etc. It is true that money may help these things happen, but money cannot *make* them happen. Money is just a tool, like a hammer is to a carpenter. A hammer has the potential to create a meaningful structure, but it takes a skilled carpenter to put it to good, productive use. When used correctly, a hammer can build a home. When used correctly, money can build security, bring financial peace, allow you to help others, and support your life aspirations. But the hammer cannot do so without your willingness to learn and then use the skills necessary to allow it to be productive.

9. IT'S NOT NICE (OR NECESSARY) TO TALK ABOUT MONEY

This is a very common money script in our culture. While there are endless hours of TV and radio shows about money, and countless books and magazines about money, in fact, talking about money and our relationship to it is one of our biggest taboos. We find it is easier for clients to talk about their sexual secrets than their money secrets! There is a saying among therapists: "You are as sick as your secrets." If we apply this saying to money, we can assume we live in a terribly sick society. The subject of money—what we believe about it, how we relate to it, how we behave with it, the secrets we keep about our own behaviors with it—is the biggest set of secrets in American life. The price we pay is that by not talking about money we restrict ourselves from learning, growing, and sharing our knowledge with our children. Our attitudes, beliefs and behaviors around money have an effect on our children much like "Trickle-Down Economic Theory." Our children's ideas, attitudes, beliefs, current and future behaviors and experiences with money are but mirrors of what they have observed from a distance and been taught by example. There are hundreds of summer camps in this country for children for developing their ballet, baseball, basketball, and music skills. We send our children to these camps knowing all the while that there is little chance our sons and daughters will be able to make a living doing these things. Yet, there is only one summer camp my staff and

I are aware of that teaches children the essentials about money, what it does, what it can do, what it can't do, and how it works, and that's Creative Wealth International (formerly *The Money Camp*). What is the message we are sending our children?

10. IF YOU ARE GOOD, THE UNIVERSE WILL SUPPLY ALL YOUR NEEDS

Dr. Ted Klontz, a founder of Klontz Kahler, identifies this as one of his own money scripts. He calls it his "twisted law of Karma." He lived many years believing that if he did the right things, for all the right reasons, then he didn't have to worry about anything, including his retirement or his future because the "good karma" would guarantee that good things would happen. After all, doesn't the Bible say not to worry, for if God cares for the sparrow, why should we worry about our needs? Again, while there is great spiritual and emotional value in doing good things for others and not worrying, it does not, by itself, guarantee a safe and secure future. Regardless of how "good" you are, your financial life will not take care of itself without effort on your part. We are surrounded by many good people who have dedicated their lives to doing the right thing for others at the right time and for the right reasons. Even so, because of a lack of planning for their future, they find themselves struggling to heat their homes, feed themselves, and can't afford to get the medical help and care they need and deserve. At first glance it would seem that "the universe" has not magically supplied all of their needs. Actually, "the universe" provides us opportunities, on a daily basis throughout our lives, to help us shape our own future. Some of these opportunities include budgeting and saving. If we fail to take advantage of these opportunities, it may seem as if the universe has failed us. Actually we have failed ourselves.

For more information about money scripts; what they are, how you can discover your own, how you can modify ones that aren't serving you, and examples of how others have rewritten their scripts and transformed their lives, read the book, *The Financial Wisdom of Ebenezer Scrooge: 5 Principles to Transform Your Relationship with Money*, available at:

www.creativewealthintl.org

A Few More Tools for Success

DECLARATIONS

Declarations are announcements you make to the world about a way you'd like to be. A declaration is somewhat like an *affirmation* except you are saying it out loud with your hand on your heart (which allows you to feel the vibration, or energy, in the declaration). An example of a declaration is, "I always pay myself first."

Declarations, like affirmations, must be personal (I), positive and present tense (not 'going to be' but 'am'). Here are some examples:

"I am a money magnet."

"I invest my money wisely."

"I put my money to work for me."

Because your subconscious mind is much more powerful than your conscious mind, at first it might object and even disagree with these statements. If you keep saying them regularly, however, eventually you will win over your subconscious mind and begin to 'act out' what you are telling yourself *about* yourself.

AFFORMATIONS

Afformations were developed by Noah St. John and are another mental tool you and your kids can use to create the lives you want. Afformations work better than affirmations because they are phrased as a question, e.g., "Why do I save 10% of my income?" or, "Why do I always make wise money choices?" In a nutshell, when you phrase your desired outcome as a question, your mind (and subconscious) goes to work figuring out how to answer the question and make it true! And they work! For more information on Afformations:

www.SuccessClinic.com/cmd.php?af=566597

Using declarations, affirmations and afformations on a daily basis is a very powerful habit for making positive, supportive changes in your life!

JUST FOR FUN!

ACROSS

2. A monetary fee, paid, or received, on something loaned out.
4. A type of retirement account that grows tax-free.
6. Something that puts money into our pocket.
7. Having the ability to buy something using someone else's money.
8. The act of putting your money to work for you.
11. Someone who has a net worth of a million dollars.
13. Things we waste our money on that either has no value or loses value once we buy it.
15. An important aspect of creating financial freedom.
16. A share of a company's profits.
17. A place where you buy stocks, bonds and mutual funds.
18. Interest earned on interest earned on your investment.
19. The philosophy that there is plenty to go around.
20. A financial power tool that helps you know where your money is.

DOWN

1. Something that takes money out of your pocket.
3. Making sure your records match the bank's records.
5. When the value of something goes up.
9. What you can do to increase your ability to create financial freedom.
10. An obligation to pay someone something.
12. The act of accumulating something, specifically money.
14. Using other people's time, energy or money to make money for yourself.

Answers are on page 212.

THE GOOSE THAT LAID THE GOLDEN EGG

Once upon a time, there was a poor farmer who worked the fields day and night, and had for many years. One day as he was walking along the road to go to the market, he came upon a goose with a broken wing inside a ditch. The poor farmer took pity on the goose and decided to take it home and nurse it back to health. So that night, the farmer put the goose in his chicken coop and went to bed.

The next morning, the farmer went to collect eggs from the chicken coop for breakfast. What do you think he found? A golden egg! The farmer took the egg in his hand, wondering if it could possibly be real gold. He found an axe and chopped the egg in half. It was gold, through and through! The farmer jumped up and yelled, "I'm rich! I'm rich! I'm rich!" He immediately went to the bank to exchange the gold for money. That day, the farmer didn't go to work—instead he bought everything he'd always wanted—a brand new tractor for his farm, new tools for his garden, an iPod to put all his music on, a laptop, a flat-screen TV and a new surround-sound system. That night the farmer went to bed and thought, "Wow, today I got to do everything I've always wanted to do and I didn't have to work. This was probably the best day of my life. I will always keep it in my memory."

The next morning the farmer went to collect eggs from his chicken coop. Lo and behold, he found another golden egg. This time the farmer didn't even have to check if the egg was real; instead he just jumped up and screamed, "I'm rich! I'm rich! I'm rich!" and ran to the bank and exchanged the gold for money. The farmer bought even more things that he wanted, including trips he'd always wanted to take and dinners he could never afford before and lots and lots of jewelry for his loving wife, and a speedboat for good measure. That night, the farmer went to bed under his brand new comforter and thought, "Wow, two days in a row where I didn't have to work and could do anything to my heart's content. I will always keep these two days in my memory."

191

The next morning, the farmer again went to collect eggs from his chicken coop. He found yet another golden egg. The day after that he also found a golden egg, and the day after that, and the day after that, and the day after that, and the day after that, and the day after that, and the day after that and this went on for quite awhile and pretty soon, the farmer became really good at spending money; so good in fact that the money was running out faster than the day. One day, the farmer had an idea. He thought to himself, "I'll bet if I went into the coop and killed the goose and gutted it, I could have all the golden eggs at once!"

The farmer went into his brand new tool shed that be bought with the golden goose egg money and grabbed the shiny new axe that he bought with his golden goose egg money and went into the new goose coop that he bought with his golden goose egg money and hoisted the axe above his head and CHOPPED the goose's head off and CLEFT the goose in half, and what do you think he found inside? Nothing but goose guts.

And so the farmer went back to working the fields day and night for the rest of his life and his wife ended up leaving him for the golden goose farmer across the street.

So what's the moral of the story? Don't kill your golden goose, especially if it's producing money you don't have to work for, and we call that passive income.

THE LANGUAGE OF MONEY

"Language is the source of misunderstandings."
~ ANTOINE DE SAINT-EXUPERY

These are basic financial terms everyone needs to understand. We've put symbols next to the words that are specific to the Three Pillars: S=Stock Market, R=Real Estate and B=Business.

401K Retirement plan offered by a for-profit company that allows its employees to set aside money tax-deferred for retirement purposes. Some companies will match employees' contributions.

ABUNDANCE The concept or belief that there is enough to go around, enough for everyone.

AMERICAN STOCK EXCHANGE (AMEX) The second-largest stock exchange in the U.S., after the New York Stock Exchange (NYSE). In general, the listing rules are a little more lenient than those of the NYSE, and thus the AMEX has a larger representation of stocks and bonds issued by smaller companies than the NYSE.

APPRECIATION Increase in value of an asset.

ASSET A valuable item that is owned.

ASSET ALLOCATION How an investor divides money into different asset classes such as stocks, bonds, cash and real estate.

AMORTIZATION The repayment of a loan in regular amounts over time.

ATM (Automated Teller Machine) CARD A plastic card issued by a bank or other financial institution to a person who has an account at that bank. It enables the account holder to deposit and withdraw money from his or her account at an ATM machine.

BALANCE The amount of money your bank statement says you have in your account at the end of each month. It doesn't reflect what's in your account right now, though!

BANK STATEMENT A form you get from the bank each month that shows you how much money you have in your account as of the date on the statement, how much you put into your account that month, how much you took out of your account that month (withdrawals, checks, ATM, debit card purchases) and any fees you paid.

BALANCE SHEET   Lists the value of assets, liabilities and the net worth of a person or company.

BEAR MARKET   A prolonged period of time during which stock prices fall accompanied by widespread pessimism. (S)

BELIEF SYSTEM   A set of facts, ideas and concepts that a person thinks is true or real. A person's belief system controls, to a large extent, his thoughts, feelings, actions and choices.

BOARD OF DIRECTORS   Individuals elected by a corporation's shareholders to oversee the management of the corporation. (B)

BOND   An investment involving lending money to governments (city or federal) or corporations. It has a face value (the amount it is worth when it matures), a fixed interest rate, and a fixed maturity date (when the bond holder receives the face value of the bond). (S)

BORROWING   Using an asset that belongs to someone else, which you must return.

BROKER   An individual or firm that acts as an intermediary between a buyer and seller, usually charging a commission. For securities and most other products, a license is required. (S)

BUDGET   A forecast of your income and expenses expected for a time frame in the future; also known as your SSP or Savings and Spending Plan.

BULL MARKET   A prolonged period in which stock prices rise faster than the historical average. (S)

CAPITAL   Wealth in the form of cash or goods, used to generate income. The net worth of a company (assets minus liabilities) is also called capital. (S,B,R)

CASH FLOW   A measure of a company's financial health. It equals cash taken in less cash paid out over a given period of time. (S,B,R)

CEO   The acronym for Chief Executive Officer—usually the president of a company. (B)

CFO The acronym for Chief Financial Officer—the executive responsible for the financial planning and record keeping for a company. (B)

CERTIFICATE OF DEPOSIT (CD) A low-risk, low-return investment offered by banks or savings and loans. It is also called a "time deposit" because the investor agrees to keep the money in the account for a specified period of time—3 months to six years. There is a monetary penalty for taking the money out before the CD's maturity.

CHARGE CARD A kind of credit card that requires you to pay the balance in full each month (for example: some American Express cards).

CHECK A form of payment for a purchase that tells the person or business to whom you wrote the check that you have the money in your account. When they deposit your check into their account, the bank will transfer that amount of money into their account to complete the purchase.

CHECKING ACCOUNT A bank account that allows you to write checks to pay for things.

COLLATERAL Property (land, house, stocks and bonds, car, jewelry, art, etc.) of value used to secure or guarantee a loan. If the loan is not paid, the lender can take the property (collateral) as payment instead.

COLLECTIBLES Items such as baseball cards, antiques, or coins that have value due to their rarity or desirability.

COMMISSION A fee charged by a broker or agent for his/her services in helping with a transaction, such as buying stock or real estate.

COMPOUND INTEREST Interest paid on the original deposit plus accumulated interest from prior periods, i.e., when your interest earns interest.

CORPORATION A form of business organization that is granted a charter by a state giving it legal rights as an entity separate from its owners. It is characterized by the limited liability of its owners and the issuance of shares of stock. (B)

CREDIT A person's ability to borrow money.

CREDIT CARD A card used to borrow money or buy goods and services, with the promise of paying later. Credit card purchases are charged interest if not paid by the due date each month.

CUSTODIAN   Agent, bank or trust company that holds and safeguards an individual's assets for them.

CUSTODIAL ACCOUNT   An account at a bank, brokerage company or other financial institution that is designed for someone under 18 years of age. This kind of account has to have a parent or guardian on the account also.

DEBIT CARD   Similar to a check, a debit card is a promise that the recipient will be paid out of your bank account immediately, electronically. As it is taken directly from funds in your bank account, no debt is incurred.

DEBT   An IOU or an obligation to pay. Bonds are debt instruments.

DEFAULT   Failure to pay back money on a timely basis that you borrowed from another.

DEPRECIATION   Decrease in value of an asset.

DEMAND   Public need or want of a product or service. Works hand in hand with "supply."

DISCOUNT BROKER   One who charges lower commission rates than a full service broker but provides fewer services such as research and advice. (S)

DIVIDEND   A portion of the profits that some companies give to their stock holders.

DIVERSIFICATION   Investing in a wide variety of investments to reduce your overall risk, since some investments may perform better than others at any given time.

DOLLAR COST AVERAGING   Investing the same amount of money on a regular schedule regardless of the price. For example, buying $25.00 worth of McDonald's stock every month. Stock prices may move up or down, but when you spread your purchases out over time, you get more shares when the price is down. Thus you buy most of your shares at a price lower than the average price. (S)

DONATION   When you give your time, energy or money to a person or organization that needs help. Donations may be tax-deductible if they are given to a public charity or nonprofit organization or 501(c)3.

DOWN PAYMENT   The part of the purchase price for a house, car or other large purchase that the buyer pays in cash, up front before he obtains a mortgage or loan on the remaining balance. Normally the larger the down payment (greater than 20%), the better the interest rate you can get on a mortgage.

DRIP (dividend reinvestment plan) A plan that automatically buys more shares of stock using dividends (profits) without paying brokerage commissions. (S)

EARNED INCOME Income from paid employment, such as wages, salaries, tips, commissions, and bonuses as opposed to income from an investment, which is unearned. Also referred to as Linear Income, which is getting paid only once on each hour you work.

EARNINGS The amount that is left of a corporation's sales (revenue) after they have paid all of their expenses.

EARNINGS PER SHARE (EPS) The total earnings of a company divided by their number of shares outstanding. EPS can be determined for any previous year (called *trailing EPS*), the current year (called *current EPS*), or for the future (called *forward EPS*). The last two would be estimates. (S)

ETF (Exchange Traded Funds) A fund that tracks an index, but can be traded like a stock. (S)

EXPENSES Things that cost you money, i.e., in a business, expenses would include office rent, paper supplies, advertising, etc. At home, expenses would include rent or your house payment, food, insurance, gas, etc. Business expenses are often tax deductible.

FDIC (Federal Deposit Insurance Corporation) An agency of the U.S. government, established in 1933, that insures deposits up to $100,000 if the bank defaults (goes out of business).

FINANCIAL FREEDOM OR INDEPENDENCE When your monthly income exceeds the monthly expenses of your chosen lifestyle. Not being dependent on anyone else for your financial expenses: housing, transportation, food, etc.

FINANCIAL PLANNER An investment professional trained to help you plan and reach your long-term financial goals through investments, tax planning, asset allocation, retirement planning, and estate planning.

FINANCIAL STATEMENT A written report that quantitatively describes your financial health at any given point in time. It includes a balance sheet: what you own (assets) minus what you owe (liabilities), and an income statement: your income and expenses. You must prepare a financial statement when you wish to qualify for a loan.

GROSS PAY The total amount of your paycheck before taxes and other deductions are taken out.

INDEX FUND A mutual fund that attempts to mimic the performance of a particular index (such as the S&P 500) by buying similar amounts of similar stocks that the index consists of. (S)

INFLATION The technical term for a rise in prices. Inflation usually occurs when there is too much money in circulation and not enough goods and services. Prices rise due to this excess demand.

INSURANCE A promise of compensation for specific potential future unexpected loss or injury in exchange for a periodic payment (e.g., health insurance, car insurance, home owner insurance, life insurance).

INTEREST 1) a fee charged by a lender for the use of borrowed money, or 2) the return on an investment.

INTEREST–COMPOUND Interest paid on the original deposit plus the accumulated interest of prior periods, i.e., when your interest makes interest.

INTEREST–SIMPLE Interest on the original deposit only.

INVESTING Putting your money to work for you through purchasing stocks, bonds, real estate or a business with the objective of making a profit (see investment).

INVESTMENT The outlay of money to purchase assets, such as stocks, bonds, real estate or a business, with the objective of making a profit when sold; or receiving an income in the form of dividends, interest, or rent while it is owned.

INVESTMENT ACCOUNT An account that generally holds securities, stocks, bonds and mutual funds.

INVESTOR One who makes a business of investing in stocks, real estate, business, etc.

IPO (Initial Public Offering) The first time a company's stock is sold to the public.

IRA (Individual Retirement Account–Traditional)   A retirement account that allows you to invest a set amount of money each year ($4000 for 2007, $5000 for 2008) where it will earn interest and/or dividends on a tax-deferred basis. You may begin withdrawing the money when you are 59½ years old. Withdrawing before that time incurs a 10% penalty.

IRS (Internal Revenue Service)   The agency that is responsible for collecting our federal income taxes.

LEVERAGE   The degree to which an investor or business is using borrowed money to operate. If a person or company is highly leveraged they run the risk of not being able to make payments on their debt.

LIABILITY or LIABILITIES (plural)   What you owe; a financial obligation or debt.

LOAN   Money or property given to a borrower with the agreement that the borrower will return the property or repay the money, usually with interest, at a specified time. (R)

MATURITY DATE   The date a loan must be paid back. (R)

MILLIONAIRE   A person whose net worth (their assets minus their liabilities, or what they own minus what they owe) is at least one million dollars

MONEY MARKET FUND   A mutual fund that buys short-term, low risk securities. The main goal is the preservation of the principal. It usually offers a higher rate of interest than bank checking or savings accounts and the money is very accessible. Most of these accounts are not FDIC insured. (S)

MORTGAGE   A legal contract between two entities providing something as collateral for a loan. Most often used when referring to real estate.

MUTUAL FUND   A fund operated by an investment company that collects money from shareholders and invests it in a group of assets as determined by that fund's objective. For example, Fidelity is an investment company and Magellan is a mutual fund with a "large growth" objective. (S)

NAIC (National Association of Investors Corporation)   A non-profit organization designed to help investors create or join investment clubs. This organization offers a variety of investment-related publications, online newsletters, software and videos that provide information on the investing process. (S)

NASDAQ **(National Association of Security Dealers Automated Quotation System)** A computerized system that facilitates the trading of stocks. Unlike the NYSE, the NASDAQ does not have a physical trading place that brings actual buyers and sellers together. (S)

NEEDS Things you have to have to live, i.e., food, water, air, transportation, housing.

NET ASSET VALUE The current market value of a single mutual fund share, calculated daily.

NET PAY The amount of your paycheck after taxes and other deductions have been taken out.

NET WORTH Total assets minus total liabilities, or what you own minus what you owe.

NO LOAD A mutual fund that does not charge a sales fee (load). (S)

NSF The acronym for insufficient funds, i.e., if you write a check and don't have enough money in your account to cover it, you will get an NSF notice from the bank and be charged NSF fees.

NYSE (New York Stock Exchange) The oldest and largest stock exchange in the United States, it still uses a large trading floor (located on Wall Street in New York City) where representatives (called brokers) of buyers and sellers conduct transactions. (S)

ONLINE BROKERAGE FIRM A stock brokerage business that is accessible online, i.e., TDAmeritrade, Scott Trade. (S)

PASSIVE INCOME Income received from business investments or real estate in which an individual is not actively involved, such as rent from an apartment building. (S, B, R)

PE RATIO (Price per Earnings Ratio) The current price of a stock (share) divided by it's earnings. For example, if a company is currently trading at $43 a share and earnings over the last 12 months were $1.95 per share, the P/E ratio for the stock would be 22.05 ($43/$1.95). (S)

PENSION A benefit (money or compensation) offered by some employers paid after a person retires. These plans generally pay you a monthly income based upon your years of service with the employer. (B)

PHILANTHROPY Contributing to the well-being of humankind by charitable aid or donations.

PIDDLYJUNK The things we buy that either goes down in value immediately (example, a car or clothing) or has no value after we purchase it (coffee, junk food).

POINTS A finance charge paid by the borrower at the beginning of a loan. One point is the same as one percent of the loan amount. (R)

PORTFOLIO A collection of one's investments (stocks, bonds, mutual funds, real estate).

PORTFOLIO INCOME The income received from the investments in a portfolio.

PRINCIPAL The amount of money borrowed or the part of the amount borrowed that is still owed. In investing, the principal is the amount of the original investment. (S, B, R)

PROFIT The money a business makes after it pays all its expenses.

PROSPECTUS A disclosure document telling the details of the mutual fund shares or stock of the company that issues it. The purpose of the prospectus information is to help an individual decide if the investment is right for him/her.

RATE OF RETURN Similar to Return on Investment (ROI), there are many different definitions of Rate of Return and Return on Investment. Basically it is the amount of money one makes on an investment, usually expressed as a percentage. (S, B, R)

RECONCILE (same as balance) To make sure your banking records (normally for a checking account) match your monthly bank statement.

REGISTER A booklet or sheet with columns and rows used to help you keep track of your spending, e.g., checks you write, debit card purchases, deposits, withdrawals, etc.

RETIREMENT The point at which a person chooses to stop working full time. The legal age to receive federal social security payments is 62 and the amount you get increases if you retire or choose to receive it at a later age.

RICH   A word some people use to describe someone or something that has a lot of value, i.e., a millionaire might be considered rich; a piece of chocolate cake might be considered rich!

ROI (Return on Investment)   The profit you make on an investment, expressed as a percentage. If you put $1000 into an investment and one year later it's worth $1,100 you have made a profit of $100. Your ROI is your profit ($100) divided by the initial investment ($1000) or 10%.

ROTH IRA   An IRA, established in the Taxpayer Relief Act of 1997, which allows taxpayers, subject to certain income limits, to save for retirement while allowing the savings to grow tax-free. Taxes are paid on contributions, but withdrawals, subject to certain rules, are not taxed at all.

RULE OF 72   The method used to determine how fast your money will double at a given interest rate. Money earning 6% will double in 12 years. 72 divided by the interest rate equals the number of years it will take for you to double your money.

SALARY   A set amount of money you are paid each month for your job.

SAVING   The act of accumulating something.

SAVINGS ACCOUNT   An account in which the money earns interest but cannot be withdrawn by check writing.

SCARCITY   An insufficient supply of something; the philosophy that there isn't enough to go around.

SECURITY   A tradable document, such as stocks or bonds, which shows evidence of debt or ownership, such as a share of a business.

SHARE (same as a stock certificate)   A certificate representing one unit of ownership in a corporation, mutual fund, or limited partnership. (S)

SOCIAL SECURITY   A government program that provides workers and their dependents with retirement income or disability income. The social security tax on wages is used to pay for this program.

SUPPLY AND DEMAND   The concept that the price of an item is determined by the point at which the quantity available (supply) equals the quantity demanded. The price of an item will usually rise if there is more demand for the item than there is quantity available (witness Tickle-Me Elmo's popularity a few years ago). Prices will usually fall if there is more of an item available than there is demand for it (the reason behind most department store sales).

STOCK An instrument that shows ownership in a corporation and represents a claim on a percentage of the corporation's assets and liabilities. The percentage is determined by the number of shares owned in relation to how many share exist. (S)

STOCK CERTIFICATE A document that represents ownership in a corporation. (S)

SYSTEM A method of doing something or creating something that leads to the same end result every time.

TAX An amount of money levied by a government on a product or a person's income. There are various kinds of taxes such as income tax, sales tax, gasoline tax, and property tax. Taxation funds government services such as road improvement, public education, and street cleaning.

TAX DEFERRED Earnings from an investment that are not taxed until the year in which you use the money (see IRA).

TAX EXEMPT (same as tax free) Earnings from an investment that are never taxed. Some cities issue bonds that earn interest tax-free.

TITHING Giving a percentage of one's income as a donation, usually on a regular basis, to a worthy cause, such as a church, a mission, or Green Peace. Also known as donating or giving or philanthropy.

TOTAL RETURN The amount received from an investment, including dividends, interest, and the appreciation or depreciation in the price, over a given period of time.

TREASURY BILLS (T-bills) United States government debt obligations that mature in one year or less and are exempt from state and local taxes. They are low risk since they are backed by the government. Bills and bonds are one way in which the government raises money for its projects.

TREASURY BONDS A coupon-bearing long-term debt instrument issued by the US government ranging from 10-30 years maturity issued in minimum denominations of $1000. Interest is paid by redeeming a coupon every six months.

VALUE The believed or perceived worth of an item. Something 'has value' or is 'valuable.'

VALUES   Usually refers to a person's morals or ethics or beliefs.

VOLATILITY   A measure of the price movement of a security or the stock market in general. If prices move up and down quickly over short periods of time, the stock has high volatility. If the price rarely changes, it has low volatility.

VOID   Empty of value or meaning; when you write a check and mess it up and need to destroy it, you write VOID in the checkbook register or sometimes write VOID on the check itself.

WALL STREET   A common name for the financial district in New York City and the street where the New York and American Stock Exchanges are located. (S)

WANTS   The things in life we don't necessarily need but have a desire for, i.e., a new bike or car, going on vacation, new clothes, a new stereo.

WITHHOLDING TAX   The amount of an employee's income that an employer sends directly to the federal and state governments as partial payment of an individual's tax liability for the year.

YIELD   The annual rate of return on an investment, expressed as a percentage, similar to ROI. (S, R, B)

Books, Games and Programs for Adults

I've heard it said that a person will remain the same throughout his lifetime except for the books he reads and the people he hangs out with. I couldn't agree more.

There are so many great financial books available for adults and kids, it's hard to list them all. Here's a few of my favorites. For more, please visit our online bookstore at:

www.creativewealthintl.org

The Millionaire Maker Game from Live Out Loud

Cash Flow Games from RichDad.com

Cash Flow Quadrant by Robert Kiyosaki

Cash Machine for Life by Loral Langemeier

Frontier Trainings with Clinton Swain

How to Profit from Credit Cards by Curtis E. Arnold

Keys to the Kingdom by Alison Armstrong (about men/women)

Multiple Streams of Income by Robert Allen

Reallionaire by Farrah Gray

Rich Dad, Poor Dad by Robert Kiyosaki

Secrets of the Millionaire Mind by T. Harv Eker

Smart Couples Finish Rich by David Bach

Smart Women Finish Rich by David Bach

The 4-Hour Work Week by Timothy Ferris

The Financial Wisdom of Ebenezer Scrooge: 5 Principles to Transform Your Relationship with Money by Ted Klontz, Ph.D., Brad Klontz, PsyD & Rick Kahler, CFP

The Little Book that Beat the Market by Joel Greenblatt

The Power of Personal Growth by Manny Goldman, founder of PersonalGrowth.com

The Millionaire Maker by Loral Langemeier

The Secrets of Money by Braun Mincher

Think and Grow Rich by Napolean Hill

Wealth Cycle Investing by Loral Langemeier

Women and Money by Kim Kiyosaki

GREAT BOOKS AND GAMES FOR KIDS

CashCow Kids: The Guide to Financial Freedom at Any Age by Lisa Jordan

Making Money by Sally Taylor

Rich Dad, Poor Dad for Teens by Robert Kiyosaki

Cash Flow for Kids Game by Robert Kiyosaki

Conductor Cash and the Prosperity Express by Kim Deep

Rich Kid, Smart Kid by Robert Kiyosaki

The Everything® Kids Money Book by Diane Mayr

The Totally New Awesome Money Book for Kids by Arthur Gochner & Rose Bochner

The Totally New Awesome Business Book for Kids by Arthur Gochner & Rose Bochner

You Call the Shots by Cameron Johnson

SAVING AND SPENDING PLAN (AKA A BUDGET)

Unless you know where you are, it's hard to know how to get where you want to go. A Savings and Spending Plan puts you in charge and gives you a tool with which to reach your dreams. Let's assume you are making $3000 a month at your first real job. Let's fill in the blanks below and get started!

Gross Income/per month
- ❏ From Job $3,000.00

Taxes/per month
- ❏ Federal, State, Social Security, Medicare (32%) . . $ 960.00

Net Income (take home pay)/per month
- ❏ Gross income minus taxes $2,040.00

Your Money Jars
- ❏ Living Jar (55%) $1,122.00
- ❏ FREEDOM Jar (10%) . . . . $ 204.00
- ❏ Saving-Contingency Jar (10%). . . . . $ 204.00
- ❏ Education Jar (10%). . . . . $ 204.00
- ❏ Play Jar (10%). . . . . $ 204.00
- ❏ Donation Jar (5%). . . . . $ 102.00

Expenses

Turn to the next page and fill in the amount you think you might spend on the expenses listed. When you have finished, add up the total and put it in the box below and subtract it from your Living expenses total. If you have money left over, good job! If you didn't have enough, you'll need to go back and look over your expenses to see where you might cut back.

Living Expenses (fill in from above): $1,122
Subtract your total expenses (from next page): . . . . . . $_____
Remainder, if any (put into your FREEDOM Jar!): . . . . . $_____

Other expenses you might not think of:

- Bank fees
- Bottled water
- Washing your car
- Dentist
- New tires
- Driver's license renewals
- Smog checks
- Laundromats
- Cover charges
- Coffee drinks/smoothies
- Gum
- Office supplies
- Emergencies
- Uniforms
- and on & on!!!

IT'S NOT AS EASY AS YOU MIGHT THINK!

TESTIMONIALS AND STORIES

We get cards, letters and emails on a regular basis containing testimonials from parents who send their kids and teens to our programs and from the adults that attend our Creative Wealth workshops. Their words just make our day and keep us getting up each morning to do it again! For a video of testimonials, please visit our home page, and be prepared to laugh! Here are some of our favorites.

"Mariano's mom (the boy that was half asleep during the workshop) thanked me/us for Money Camp. After her son debriefed his parents about what was covered at camp, they purchased another house as rental property and said it is the best investment ever!" The teacher of the camp added in her email to us, *"I guess he was paying attention."*

~ SAUNDRA ANDERSON, CREATIVE WEALTH COACH IN SAN FRANSISCO.

"It was the third, intense night of what I can only describe as a never-ending, more-than-money, raw-energy high. Ms. E had asked her attentive, Train-the-Trainer audience to share a memory . . . about money. The kinesthetic, or is it visual, part of me looked upward to recall forgotten memories of my childhood. I distinctly remembered the smirk that formed on my face as I recalled the facts of my 6th grade year of middle school. There were few moments that I could actually recall being "happy times," but the one that stood out for me was a red 10-speed bike that step-dad bought. I used to ride that bike through the neighborhood . . . a very rare time when this old tired body actually exercised. It was freedom. An escape from my premature exposure to real world problems. And one day . . . the red bike was gone. Without warning. Without explanation. Gone. Long after crossing into adulthood, I found out that step-dad had pawned that red bike, undoubtedly, to help himself out of one of his many financial binds. For me, the recollection of this event was nothing more than my introduction to hocking items to pay bills. Ms. E, the universal lady, however extracted a far deeper metaphor. She shared her two cents on just how that particular experience has shaped my entire being . . . of mistakenly being labeled as selfish. Frugal. Tight with my money. It was during the moments of her feedback, that I instantaneously discarded those labels put on me. No one had ever seen it [as she had] before. And just like any emotional release . . . I started to feel the stinging tears well up in the bottom of my eyes. And then that peace that surpasses all understanding came over me. There it was

209

again. Freedom. I didn't need the red bike anymore . . . for I had learned the bigger lesson. Peace and love to you always, Ms. E."

~ BRETTA GRANT-TAYLOR, CREATIVE WEALTH COACH

"It's amazing what we hear about the Money Camp program here in Brazil. It comes through parents, specialists, schools. Our first Money Camp children are very special. They started the program in March 2007 and they will finish in December 2007. They tell us the program is already affecting their lives.

Joaõ Vítor is an 11-year-old kid and his example really motivates us to continue. His aunt told us that last month she paid some bills with the credit card and that she was going to pay the bills again with the credit card and João said to her, "Hey. Are you going to pay the bills with the credit card again? Don't you remember that you did not pay the full credit card invoice? This is not correct. You first should pay the total amount and then use it again!"

Nathan is one of our 10-year-old Money Camp students. He asked us, "Guess what I asked my dad for, for Children's Day?" Since he's a kid we thought he would ask for an iPod or a new Play Station. We were really surprised that he asked for a savings account to start on the road to his future! And then we thought, what a wonderful job we are doing!

Another kid, Enzo, is also 10 years old. His family moved to the countryside last July, during school holidays here in Brazil. His mommy said he was really excited about the holidays. As they were moving they spent a lot of money refurbishing the new house and buying new furniture. They asked Enzo if he wanted to travel during the holidays as he is used to doing. Mommy and Daddy were surprised when Enzo told them, "I know we are buying a new house and it costs lots of money. If you think my holiday trip is not going to surpass your budget, OK, but if you think we should wait for next year, it is OK with me." Mom came to us and said, "Thank you for what Money Camp is doing for my family!"

"The Money Camp arrival in Brazil in 2007 was very opportune. There is a lack of a financial literacy programs for kids in our country. I've been searching and working on financial materials focusing on children's education for awhile, and I have not found a program that is so well structured. Schools that adopt the program will be able to accelerate the introduction of this fundamental theme of citizenship. Certainly, the children educated in this program will catch a glimpse of a different future; one that is much

more promising. There's no magic at all! It's just a question of helping kids to see some issues and behaviors related to finance in a much clearer way than many adults do. And the best thing of all is that they are learning by playing, in a natural and funny way. Welcome to Brazil, Money Camp! Our schools and families are grateful for the initiative."

~ SENT TO US BY SILVIA ALAMBERT, MONEY CAMP LICENSEE IN BRAZIL.

"Money talks. Getting a regular, dependable allowance is essential for a kid, not a luxury. Managing an allowance empowers, increases confidence, and reminds me that I'm deserving of my Mom's trust. I've never complained that it's not enough. Rather, when I wanted more, I started my own business with the tools I learned from Money Camp."

~ ANDREW ADAMS, 14, HAS ATTENDED 3 MONEY CAMPS

"I'll vouch for Creative Wealth's teaching, as well. I attended a train-the-trainer event with them last year, and had a chance to see what they're doing and developing to effectively reach youth and adults. Amazing information and training techniques that are a quantum leap over other curriculum and teaching methods. Impossible to be bored, even for teenagers with 'tude. In addition, if any members are considering sending their kids, they should really consider going with them – they will also benefit tremendously from attending, and the first adult is free with student."

~ CHRIS GEROW, OPERATIONS MANAGER, FAITH BASED FCU, SAN DIEGO COUNTY'S ONLY LOW-INCOME, COMMUNITY DEVELOPMENT CU

ANSWERS TO CROSSWORD PUZZLE, PAGE 190

ACROSS

2.	Interest
4.	ROTHIRA
6.	Asset
7.	Credit
8.	Investing
11.	Millionaire
13.	Piddlyjunk
15.	Planning
16.	Dividend
17.	Stockmarket
18.	Compound
19.	Abundance
20.	Budget

DOWN

1.	Liability
3.	Reconcile
5.	Appreciation
9.	Education
10.	Loan
12.	Saving
14.	Leverage

TESTIMONIALS FROM KIDS AND TEENS

We get great cards, letters and emails containing testimonials via from parents who send their kids and teens to our programs. Some of them just make our day! For a video of testimonials, please visit our home page, and be prepared to laugh! Here are some of our favorites.

The most valuable thing I learned was that becoming a millionaire is a choice, not a dream.—KATIE

The most valuable thing I learned was to start saving early and to let the money do the work for you. It was SO much better than I expected and it was the most fun I've ever had while learning.— TIFFANY

Money Camp has been the best week of my summer. I really appreciated coming and would do it again if I could.—CARTER

The most valuable thing I learned was how to not only manage and budget, but also to make my money grow.—IMANI

The most valuable thing I learned was that I can start right now to make money.—PAMELA

The most valuable thing I learned was that I can start investing at any age and the earlier the better.—JENNIFER

It was really fun. I am going to start managing and planning what to do with my money.—AARON

Money Camp was really fun! I learned a lot about money. These ideas will help me a lot through my lifetime.—ANUJ

The most valuable thing I learned was that being a millionaire is a choice. I loved this camp. It was so fun!—NOREEN

Thank you!! I learned a lot and everyone was energetic. I will be sure to come back next year.—ESTEPHEN

Answers to the Magic of Compound Interest Activity (page 128):

10% Interest = $756,979, 12% Interest = $1,709.453

From page 181

The best choice? If you took the penny,
at the end of 30 days you'd have

$5,368,709.12!

CREATIVE WEALTH PRINCIPLE
Pay Yourself First!

INDEX

M

metaphors

for approaching life 113

"The Goose that Laid the
Golden Egg" 191–192

money 71. *See also* money
personalities; *See
also* money scripts

accumulation of vs. utilization of 151

attitudes toward, boys vs.
girls 120

belief systems regarding
59–61, 76–77

definition of 14

and education 31, 32, 42

glossary of terms related to
187–198

running out of, responding
to 136–137

spread 154

stereotypes regarding
53–55

worksheet for determin-
ing 54–55

Money Jars 70–86, 90–93.
See also Donation Jar;
See also Education Jar;

See also Living Jar;
See also Freedom Jar;
See also Play Jar; *See
also* Savings Jar

allocating funds to 82–84,
97–98

earned income and 154

for adults 81

for couples 81–82

questions regarding 79–82

unexpected income and
83

using bank accounts in-
stead of 80–81

money personalities 56–59,
165–167

the amasser 58, 167

the avoider 58, 176

the binger 176

the monk 58, 176

the saver/hoarder 57, 165

the spender 57, 165–166

the worrier 58, 167

worksheet for determining
58–59

money scripts 173–178

Great Gifts for Family & Friends

ONLINE: www.Creativewealthintl.com
BY PHONE: 800-928-1932/805-957-1024
BY MAIL: Creative Wealth Intl., LLC
135 Chapala Street, Santa Barbara, CA 93101
BY FAX: 805-957-0125

Qty	Item	Price	Total
____	*Ultimate Allowance Book (print)*	*$24.95 ea.*	$ _____
____	*Ultimate Allowance Book (download PDF)*	*$24.95 ea.*	$ _____
____	*Creative Cash for Kids (print)*	*$69.00 ea.*	$ _____
____	*Creative Cash for Kids (download PDF)*	*$29.00 ea.*	$ _____
____	*Life's Little Wealth Principle Cards (adult)*	*$19.95 ea.*	$ _____
____	*Sammy's It's a Habit Music CD*	*$10.00 ea.*	$ _____
____	*Sammy's It's a Habit Music CD (download)*	*$10.00 ea.*	$ _____
____	*It's a Habit, Sammy Rabbit! book*	*$8.95 ea.*	$ _____
____	*Sammy's "Will Sammy Ride..."*	*$8.95 ea.*	$ _____
	Sales Tax (CA ship to addresses only at 8.75%)*		$ _____
	Shipping Charges (see box below)		$ _____
		GRAND TOTAL	$ _____

* There is no sales tax on downloadable products.

PAYMENT METHOD: ❏ *Visa/MC/AMX* ❏ *Check/Money Order*

Card number:_____Ex. Date:_____
Name on Card:_____
Billing Address:_____
Signature:_____CVV Code:_____

SHIP TO:

Name: _____
Street Address: _____
City, State, Zip:_____
Phone:_____
Email:_____

S & H:
• 1 item   *$5.00*
• 2-5 items   *$10.00*
• 6-10 items   *$14.95*
No shipping on PDFs
Call for Overnight Rates

Prices are subject to change.

www.ingramcontent.com/pod-product-compliance
Lightning Source LLC
LaVergne TN
LVHW011223080426
835509LV00005B/291